MEANINGFUL MOMENTS IN MINISTRY

50 YEARS, 20 DENOMINATIONS

Rev. John W. Friesen, Ph.D., D.Min., D.R.S.

Copyright © 2014 by Rev. John W. Friesen, Ph.D., D.Min., D.R.S.

First Edition – July 2014

ISBN

978-1-4602-2111-2 (Hardcover)

978-1-4602-2112-9 (Paperback)

978-1-4602-2113-6 (eBook)

All rights reserved.

No part of this publication may be reproduced in any form, or by any means, electronic or mechanical, including photocopying, recording, or any information browsing, storage, or retrieval system, without permission in writing from the publisher.

Cover Design by David J Friesen

Produced by:

FriesenPress

Suite 300 – 852 Fort Street

Victoria, BC, Canada V8W 1H8

www.friesenpress.com

Distributed to the trade by The Ingram Book Company

CONTENTS

PREFACE xi

INTRODUCTION 1
    INITIAL EXPERIENCES
    TRAINING FOR MINISTRY
    PARENTAL INFLUENCE

PART ONE: VIGNETTES OF MINISTRY 7
   I. BEGINNINGS: FAMILY EXPERIENCES AND INSIGHTS 9
      SUMMER CAMP EXPERIENCES
      STREET VAGABONDS
      FINDING THE LORD'S WILL:
      IT MAY HAVE WORKED FOR GIDEON
      PLAYING POSITIVES
      VARYING PERSPECTIVES
      IMPORTANCE OF EDUCATION
      PROFESSIONAL QUALIFICATIONS
      A SUPPORTIVE ROLE?
      GETTING IT RIGHT

   II. INITIAL PASTORAL EXPERIENCES 23
      MY CALL TO PREACH
      YOU FORGOT THE OFFERING!
      UNOFFICIAL CHURCH FUNCTIONARIES

    BUSY PASTORAL SCHEDULE

    SLEEPING SAM

    TEA FOR TWO

    A GIFT FROM THE MEN OF BONANZA

    A BRIEF, SWEET GIFT

    BY JOHN W. FRIESEN, WRITTEN IN HONOUR OF GARY LYNCH

    JACOB'S ACRE

    A CONFERENCE DILEMMA

    PROFESSIONAL JEALOUSY?

    BAPTISM SECRET

    SETTLING DISPUTES

    MY FIRST CHURCH CONFLICT

    PRISON TIME

    COMMITTED STEWARDSHIP?

    SETTING MINISTERIAL PRIORITIES

    MY FIRST ALTAR CALL

    MY VERY BRIEF BASEBALL CAREER

III. DEFINING MOMENTS IN MINISTRY 49

    A POTPOURRI OF LEARNED LESSONS

    THE EXCITING SIXTIES

    THE SPOILED BRAT

    DIVORCE COUNSELING

    ENCOUNTER WITH A CULT

    MY NEARLY GAMBLING CAREER

    A QUARTET SERMON

    A PROMISING PASTOR IN TRAINING

    THE STONE WAS ROLLED AWAY

IV. PRAYER 63

    COMMENTS ON PRAYER

    GOD ANSWERS PRAYER

    CONTRACT PRAYER

    PARADOXICAL USE OF PRAYER

    A NEW MAKE OF LAWNMOWER

THE RIGHT PLACE AT THE RIGHT TIME

A GRATEFUL RECIPIENT OF PRAYER

V. LOVE AND MARRIAGE 73

DETAILS, DETAILS

IMPROMPTU ACT

TRUE LOVE

MARRIAGE IS A SERIOUS BUSINESS

MINISTER FOR HIRE?

CAREFUL PLANNING

SOLEMNITY EXCLUDED

LET'S GET MARRIED—NOW!

A MOUNTAINTOP WEDDING

A TRULY INTERFAITH WEDDING

A DIFFERENT INTERFAITH WEDDING

THE WEDDING I FORGOT

VI. SAYING GOODBYE 89

MY FIRST FUNERAL

ASSISTANT FUNERAL DIRECTOR

AN IMPRESSIVE FUNERAL

LOYALTY AMID TRAGEDY

A RURAL CHRISTIAN STALWART

ODE TO UNCLE HENRY

VII. DIVERSITY IN MINISTRY 99

AH, THOSE COUNTRY CHRISTIANS!

MULTICULTURALISM IN ITS INFANCY

ETHNIC INVASION

ENCOUNTER WITH PREJUDICE

INSIGHTS FROM THE DOUKHOBORS

IT'S OUR TRADITION

REVERENCE FOR SACRED WRITINGS

UNDESERVED FORGIVENESS

TRUE FAMILY WORSHIP

GRANDPA, GRANDPA; LOOK AT ALL THE INDIANS!

EVERYBODY SING

I WANT TO GIVE YOU SOMETHING

PART TWO: UNFOLDING OF MY MINISTERIAL CAREER..................117

DENOMINATION NO. 1:
GOSPEL HALL (PLYMOUTH BRETHREN) 119

DENOMINATION NO. 2:
THE SALVATION ARMY 123

DENOMINATION NO. 3:
PRESBYTERIAN CHURCH IN CANADA 125

DENOMINATION NO. 4:
FULL GOSPEL CHURCH 127

DENOMINATION NO. 5:
PENTECOSTAL ASSEMBLIES OF CANADA 129

DENOMINATION NO. 6:
THE CHRISTIAN AND MISSIONARY ALLIANCE 131

DENOMINATION NO. 7:
SEVENTH-DAY ADVENTIST CHURCH IN CANADA 135

DENOMINATION NO. 8:
ANGLICAN CHURCH OF CANADA 137

DENOMINATION NO. 9:
WILLIAM ABERHART'S INDEPENDENT BAPTIST CHURCH ... 139

DENOMINATION NO. 10:
THE CHURCH OF GOD (ANDERSON, INDIANA) 141

DENOMINATION NO. 11:
MENNONITE CHURCH CANADA
(FORMERLY, GENERAL CONFERENCE MENNONITE CHURCH)
.... 145

DENOMINATION NO. 12:
THE MENNONITE BRETHREN CHURCH 147

DENOMINATION NO. 13:

THE BAPTIST UNION 155

DENOMINATION NO. 14:
THE EVANGELICAL UNITED BRETHREN CHURCH 157

DENOMINATION NO. 15:
THE UNITED METHODIST CHURCH 163

DENOMINATION NO. 16:
THE EVANGELICAL CHURCH IN CANADA 165

DENOMINATION NO. 17:
THE FREE METHODIST CHURCH 169

DENOMINATION NO. 18:
THE EVANGELICAL LUTHERAN CHURCH 171

DENOMINATION NO. 19:
THE ROMAN CATHOLIC CHURCH 173

DENOMINATION NO. 20:
THE UNITED CHURCH OF CANADA 175

PART THREE: POEMS FOR REFLECTION **179**

PRAYER 181

THE MODEL PREACHER 183

THANKS, I'D RATHER NOT! 185

THE CRISIS IN PREACHING 187

SUNDAY CHURCH 189

BLESSINGS OF WORSHIP 191

SINGING LIFTS THE SOUL 193

TEACHING SUNDAY SCHOOL 195

PARTIAL THINGS 197

THE LORD'S PRAYER 199

A TIME ALONE 201

A PRAYER FOR COMMUNION 203

BECAUSE HE'S GOD 205

AN EASTER PRAYER	207
THE BIG QUESTION	209
THE LIFE CYCLE	211
A CREED FOR YOUTH	213
A TRIBUTE	215
DEAR MOM	217
DAD'S 90TH BIRTHDAY	219
I MET GOD	221
EPILOGUE	223
ABOUT THE AUTHOR	225

To my beloved wife,
Virginia Agnes Lyons Friesen
My partner in everything

PREFACE

Like most clergymen, I like to tell stories; we call them *illustrations* in the profession, and often they are drawn on to explain sermon points. Sometimes these stories come from real life—often from a previous ministerial assignment, while at other times they are simply known as "stories preachers tell."

I had the good fortune of enjoying my fifty plus years in ministry, even though those years included both ups and downs. The stories in this collection describe some of my experiences, and all of them are true! However, Some sermon illustrations included here, while humourous and often related by clergymen, are probably not grounded in fact. Here are three examples of that kind of story.

> A couple approached the minister before the morning worship service began and asked him if he would marry them as soon as possible. The couple, with a marriage license in hand, seemed to be in a hurry to get it done. The minister agreed to perform the ceremony, but suggested that the couple wait until after the service when he would make the announcement and they could come forward to the front of the church to be married. After some discussion, the prospective bride and groom concurred with the minister's suggestion.
>
> As the service ended, the minister did as he promised,

and intoned; "Would the man and woman who want to be married please come forward."

The congregation was shocked when one man and eleven women stood to make their way to the altar!

* * *

About a century ago the minister of a small backwoods congregation was approached by a couple who wanted to be married. They appeared to have the proper legal documents in order and were accompanied by two witnesses. Although it was Sunday, the weekly church service had ended, so the minister declared himself ready to proceed.

The wedding ceremony was rather brief since there was no accompanying music and no guests to greet. As the newlyweds prepared to leave, the groom turned to the minister and inquired into the cost of the ceremony.

"I don't usually charge for conducting a wedding ceremony," the minister replied. "But you can make a donation to the church if you like. It's entirely up to you."

The new husband carefully counted out five crisp new one-dollar bills, then taking a lingering look at his new wife, he promptly retrieved two of the one-dollar bills and put them back into his pocket!

* * *

There are times, even in ministry, when personal egos rise up unexpectedly, even in ministry, and this happened to a young clergyman in his first pastoral charge. Whenever a parishioner said something positive about his sermons or personage, he repeated the comment to his wife—sometimes more than once. A parishioner might observe that a particular sermon "hit the spot," or the minister "told it like it was," or the minister should be regarded as a "model preacher." Naturally, the minister would later repeat the compliments to his spouse.

However, on occasion, it simply became just a little too much for his poor wife.

One Sunday morning after the worship service was over, and the minister was at the door shaking hands with parishioners, an elderly woman looked him in the eye and told him he was "a warm preacher." Naturally, he relayed what he thought was a compliment to his wife several times during the following week. When she had had enough of it, the preacher's wife told her husband to look up the word "warm" in the dictionary.

He did so and what he discovered somewhat shook him up. The definition of "warm" read, "not too hot!"

* * *

Please read on; the following stories from my *50 years, 20*

Rev. John W. Friesen, Ph.D., D.Min., D.R.S. xiii

denominations are true!

John W. Friesen
Calgary, Alberta
2014

MEANINGFUL MOMENTS IN MINISTRY

50 YEARS, 20 DENOMINATIONS

1

INTRODUCTION

*There's nothing a man can do to improve himself
as much as writing his memoirs. -Anonymous*

Although I had this project in mind for a long time, I actually began this book a few years ago in Florence, Italy because my eldest son, Bruce, told me it was time to get started as he handed me a beautiful leather-bound book of blank pages. The book was a souvenir from his trip to the market that afternoon. He was undoubtedly motivated by my having reached the biblical age of life expectancy—threescore and ten and…. It also occurred to me that he wanted me to start writing before I lost my memory! When he presented the book to me, he indicated that he had heard enough about my ministerial experiences, and he thought it was time for someone else to read about them. He encouraged me to start to writing, and so I began. This book is the result.

I was born in a rural shack near Waldheim, Saskatchewan, the second son of Gerhard and Barbara (nee Reimer) Friesen. I graduated from public schools and postsecondary institutions in British Columbia, Saskatchewan, Manitoba, Kansas, North Carolina, and Indiana, having earned a total of seven degrees. What can I say? I love studying.

I have gained immense pleasure from this writing experience, but I did suffer some difficulty in knowing when to stop. Each thought gave rise to a related memory and I struggled to describe each experience fully, in as few words as possible. Although I have written dozens of books, this is the only one I intend to read and reread because it contains many precious memories of meaningful experiences and refers to many individuals who greatly contributed to my own spiritual growth. I can only hope that it assists readers in revisiting their own spiritual journeys.

INITIAL EXPERIENCES

I wanted to enter the ministry as far back as I can remember. I believe I was "called to preach" at the age of six, even before I fully understood what it meant to be a Christian. I recall attending a series of tent meetings in Trail, British Columbia, with my parents during which services the evangelist delivered a message on Luke 18:9-14, a passage from the Bible that documents the praying habits of a self-righteous Pharisee and a humble tax collector. The preacher emphasized that when the tax collector prayed, he did not look up to the heavens, as the Pharisee did when *he* delivered his self-righteous monologue to the Lord. Because he was a humble penitent man, the tax collector instead bowed his head to God, beat on his chest, and asked God to forgive his sins.

Thoroughly convinced that my own sinful condition was analogous to that of the tax collector, I returned home from the meeting, knelt by my bedside, beat upon my chest, and asked Jesus to forgive my sins. Unaware that a six-year-old could have assurance of salvation, I remained in this state of uncertainty for the next two years. I will say more about this later.

A few months later, during Bible study in a Sunday school class, I came upon this verse, "Seek ye first the kingdom of God, and his righteousness; and all these things shall be added unto you" (Matthew 6:33 KJV). I was hooked; this was going to be *my* text! I became convinced that if I trusted God to supply my needs I would be freed to respond to any call of ministry and God would take care of my needs. Ironically, on reaching adulthood I never *did* enter full-time congregational ministry, but spent more than fifty fulfilling years participating in an official part-time capacity.

TRAINING FOR MINISTRY

During my Bible college and university years, I discovered there was a special need for pastors to assist with planting new churches or help out small country parishes that could not afford to call a full-time minister. After due consideration, I decided that this would be my niche—to support myself financially and be freed up to serve as a part-time minister to some needy congregation. This form of ministry would be my way of "seeking first the kingdom of God," and through God's supplying of my outside employment would "add all the other things."

Fifty years in the ministry passed quickly, and so my wife, Virginia, and I sometimes feel that it is time to let someone else take our place at our present parish. I am a bit uneasy about making such a decision, mainly because I would miss the activity of preparing sermons and delivering them. The fact that I have always enjoyed speaking before an audience sometimes make me wonder if I should perhaps have become an entertainer, an actor, or even a stage comedian. Come to think of it, there *is* much about ministry that resembles the field of drama (hint: watch any television evangelist!).

To "keep up with the times," in 2007 I completed an M.A. degree program in pastoral ministry with my Alma Mater, Trinity Theological Seminary in Newburgh, Indiana. Once again, I discovered the discipline of having to write theological papers and meet deadlines to remind myself what young seminarians go through. I told my friends that I enrolled in the program to discover what I did wrong over the previous 50 years!

One night I had a dream that helped me make peace with the decision at least to reduce my preaching load. I dreamed of King David and how in his twilight years he wanted to build a temple for God. God told him not to; someone else could do the job much better (2 Samuel 7:12-13) I decided to agree with God. Since I made that decision, it has become much easier to concentrate on my sunset years as a part-time preacher. I have also begun to view my fellow ministers in a more sympathetic way because I know what their responsibilities are with regard to administration, committee meetings, conference boards, home visitation, and preaching, as well as having personal and family responsibilities. I am finding that I pray for them more often than I used to.

During my seminary studies I completed a course entitled, Dealing With Difficult People in the Church, and discovered that nearly two-thirds of the pastors in America have been fired at least once, and 43% of those were ousted by a dissident group of ten or less. Many of these ministers do not return to the ministry. This reality has certainly influenced the way I now view the ministry. It is indeed a high calling, but it also offers some real *ups and downs* in terms of one's own spiritual journey. Let me illustrate. Not long ago, a friend called me about a "problem" they were having in their church. It seems that the minister was doing a satisfactory job, but his wife apparently seemed less than enthusiastic as her husband about the work of the church. The word "on the street" was that she sometimes even missed Sunday morning worship services and a group of "concerned" individuals (of whom my friend was one), were considering giving the minister his walking papers! As I hung up the telephone, I wondered if the minister's contract included special congregational responsibilities for his wife to fulfill. I also wondered if the minister's wife was sensing the lack of congregation's support for her role. I included that pastor's name in my next prayer!

PARENTAL INFLUENCE

I must confess to one important matter. I can honestly say that because of my extremely varied church background, I have very little specific denominational loyalty. There is no doubt that I picked up this attitude from my church-wandering parents. They seemed to follow the Holy Spirit from one denomination to another. My Dad had a unique attitude toward church even though he rarely missed a Sunday service during his entire 93 years on earth. Thanks to his commitment, we were never late for church, but our family was nearly always the first to arrive at church, often getting there even before the minister.

Dad's motto was, "If you are on time, you are late!"

Our family was also always the first to leave the churchyard after worship much to the chagrin of my brother, David, and myself. We would have preferred to linger a bit and spend some time with our teenage peers. Dad's explanation for our quick exit was this; "Leave church early; that way you won't spoil your blessing by talking with others!" He and mother also believed that if a church did not suit their needs, they would go elsewhere, even if it meant changing denominations. They did that a lot, by the way.

My parents were very loyal about two things. The first being their love for each other. The second was meeting their obligations to one another. This made it even more entertaining to tease them about being illegally wed, because their real names were Gerhard and Barbara, yet their marriage registration read George and Berbie. Mom did not like the name "Gerhard," so she always called Dad, "George," and "Berbie" was Mom's nickname. Therefore, those were the names, which the minister used on their marriage registration. Despite this mix-up of proper names on their marriage certificate, their faithfulness and loyalty to one another persisted.

Some years ago when my parents were leaving the church foyer, Dad was helping Mom with her coat, and an observer remarked, "Your husband seems so attentive; is this your second marriage?"

Rev. John W. Friesen, Ph.D., D.Min., D.R.S.

"Oh no," Mom replied, "He has been doing this for 65 years!"

They were a couple who remained entirely devoted to each other. Their marriage lasted 67 years, to the day Dad died in July 1997, a little more than a month away from his 94th birthday. They may have been free thinkers—denominationally speaking—but their marriage was in a sacred, untouchable category by itself.

Perhaps the downside to having a philosophy of cavalier denominational loyalty is that several of my siblings and I, no doubt influenced by our parents, also have no particularly strong doctrinal, denominational, or ethnic historical preferences. Some might say that this is unfortunate, but I personally enjoy being free of too many institutional encumbrances. My primary loyalty is to God through the mediation of our Lord Jesus Christ.

Perhaps it is time now to offer a series of varied anecdotal experiences that made up my fifty-year sojourn as a clergyman. It is my hope that readers will enjoy the adventures I experienced in my spiritual journey and perhaps gain encouragement from them.

John W. Friesen
University of Calgary
2014

PART ONE:
VIGNETTES OF MINISTRY

During my recent seminary studies, I concluded that congregational ministry has certainly changed over my 50 years in that role. Instead of studying the Bible and drawing out theological truths, seminarians like myself were taking courses with these titles: "Managing Conflict, Dealing with Difficult People," and "Principles of Church Discipline."

I began to wonder if I would even have entered the ministry if these courses had been offered when I was a student in Bible College! As is probably the case with many ministers, I have often encountered perplexing one-on-one situations for which I was not prepared. On the other hand, having taken these courses, I am not sure that anyone can really be prepared for some of the more challenging situations I will describe in this section.

Part One of this book consists of some of the more amusing, memorable, and enriching experiences that I will treasure for a long time. I have also included a few that I will try to put behind me!

I.
BEGINNINGS:
FAMILY EXPERIENCES AND INSIGHTS

SUMMER CAMP EXPERIENCES

The habit of sending children to church camp undoubtedly started as soon as the concept of camping was invented. The rationale for this phenomenon was apparently to have someone else teach children things they could not learn at home. I sometimes believe (and this may sound a bit cynical), that summer camps were invented to provide a week of low-cost babysitting for couples who would not otherwise be able to afford the luxury of a week's vacation without their offspring!

During the forties, when my family had a four-year affiliation with the Trail Plymouth Brethren congregation, my brother, David, and I attended their summer camp (Camp Robson), for four summers. I have fond memories of summer camp, despite the fact that I nearly cut off my index finger at breakfast just prior to our trip to the first day of camp in the first year. I was excited about going to camp. Blood spurted from the wound and my mother tied a very tight bandage around my finger to stop the bleeding. When we arrived at camp, the staff nurse examined my wound, and bandaged it, then declared that I would not be required to wash dishes for the whole week. Imagine my joy; washing dishes was a dreaded compulsory duty for every camper, and I was excused! Despite my injury, however, I was able to take copious notes during Bible classes and even won first prize for producing the best notebook.

Our camp director was a lay preacher named Roland Savage, a man very committed to his calling. In addition to taking responsibility for providing spiritual activities such as daily chapel and Bible study, he also undertook a variety of menial tasks. For example, each day he would navigate a rowboat to the other side of the lake where a dairy was located, and pick up the camp's supply of milk. He always took a few campers with him on the boat ride so he could speak with them about the Gospel. One day he invited my brother and me to join him, and because it sounded a bit more like an order than an invitation, we quickly obliged. Halfway across the lake, Mr. Savage pulled the oars into the boat and paused. Solemnly he asked us if we had wanted to "get saved." Naturally we did, not sure of how we were going to get back to shore if we did not concede.

Joking aside, it was a memorable experience, since my brother and I had been to many revival services with our parents in the past and we were quite prepared to have Mr. Savage pray with us and, "let Jesus into our hearts."

There was a lighter side to summer camp at Camp Robson. Roland Savage's wife, whose name I do not remember, served as head camp cook. Mrs. Savage would call her husband to the camp kitchen whenever she needed his services. When she issued the call, she always called "Rollie," in a high-pitched, distinct, falsetto voice. Soon pretty well every boy in camp was practicing saying "Rollie" in the cabins after quiet had been announced. Most boys were able to mimic the same sound that Mrs. Savage uttered, and everyone would laugh. My, but boys were naughty in those days! Such activities were considered juvenile delinquency in my day!

Another Camp Robson experience that stands out has to do with a renegade camper named Eddie. Eddie did not conform to camp rules, tried to avoid chapel services, and even stole another boy's property. When caught red-handed for the latter deed, he readily admitted to his crime and promptly was awarded five dollars by Mr. Savage for telling the truth. The lesson was lost on the rest of us as we talked about the event for the rest of the week, wondering if it might not be profitable to steal someone else's property, admit to the crime, and obtain a rich reward. Five dollars was a lot of money back then!

Eddie left camp a day or two earlier than the rest of the campers. It seems that his numerous misdemeanors were finally seen as negatively affecting the other campers and his parents were contacted to come and take him home. It was late in the evening when Eddie departed, and when he left the cabin one of his cohorts who was allowed to stay behind, called out, "Eddie, I hate to see you go and leave me behind with all of these Christians!" I remember being royally appalled by such apostasy.

STREET VAGABONDS

Laws about children's rights were scarce when I was a young child. Looking back at my own family's experience, I sometimes wonder how my parents got away with some of their actions. Here is a case in point.

My brother and sister, Norman and Nancy, are twins who were born a few years after we moved to British Columbia in 1936. My mother went to the Trail hospital for their birth. For some reason my parents were either not able to afford a babysitter or chose not to arrange for one.

During the time of my mother's hospital stay, my eight-year-old brother, David and I (age six) lived in our family automobile for a week. Each day of Mother's hospital stay, Dad parked the car on a downtown street, just below the window of Mom's hospital bed. Sometimes Mom would show her face at the window and wave to us, but nothing could compensate for the loss of her presence.

Each morning Dad packed a lunch for us and went off to work at the *Canadian Mining and Smelting Company* plant. He met us at the car at the end of the day, paid a brief visit to mother, and then he took the two of us home. My brother and I were told not to wander the streets during the day, but stay near or in the car.

Today this arrangement undoubtedly would be called child neglect. I have no idea as to what this experience taught me, but I remember many of the details to this day. It was not a very happy time, and when Mother finally came home, accompanied by two little babies, I could not associate the two items. I *do* remember feeling quite neglected when those two little beings invaded my six-year private space. I also recall mourning, for some time, the temporary loss of my mother.

I consider this an appropriate illustration of when I can say that I am glad the "good ole days" are gone.

FINDING THE LORD'S WILL: IT MAY HAVE WORKED FOR GIDEON

A half-century ago, Bible colleges could be described as factories of literal biblical interpretation. Not only were we taught to become "crowded to Christ," we were also tuned to expect miracles, get direct answers to prayer, and become recipients of recipes pointing out God's will for our daily lives. When it came to choosing a life's career, however, we were quite conditioned as males to become pastors, teachers, or farmers. Women could expect to serve God as nurses or teachers before they became committed wives and mothers.

Most everyone raised in a Christian church is familiar with Gideon's experience in finding the Lord's will for his life (Judges 6:36-40). The Book of Judges records that since Israel did evil in the sight of God their enemies, the Midianites, became oppressive, and God raised up a deliverer for the Israelites in the form of a humble, shy farmer named Gideon. In order to assure himself that leading Israel into battle was the will of God for his life, Gideon put God to the test. First, he asked God to put dew onto a sheep's fleece he placed on the ground, but there was to be no dew *on* the ground. When God did as Gideon requested, Gideon then reversed his request. Now he wanted dew on the ground, but not on the fleece. Once again, God acquiesced to Gideon's request.

12   Meaningful Moments in Ministry

Now it was time to go to battle, God's will was clear, and so Gideon went to war.

When I was studying at Bethany Bible College in Saskatchewan, a fellow student named Sam was torn between preparing for the ministry and choosing a teaching career. His way of testing God about the matter was to apply to both a Bible college and a teacher training institution on the same day. He prayed over the matter, and then mailed both applications. His reasoning was that he would choose whichever institution was first to send a letter of acceptance.

As it happened, a letter of acceptance from *both* institutions arrived in the mail on the same day! Now poor Sam was in a dilemma; he had no "Plan B."

After considering the matter, Sam enrolled in another Bible college and remained there for one year. However, as he was preparing to attend teachers' college he suddenly took a position as a furniture salesman, a career he consequently held for nearly forty years, eventually even becoming store manager.

Who says that the Lord does not work in mysterious ways?

Based on my friend Sam's experience, I concluded that Gideon's approach does not literally work for everyone!

PLAYING POSITIVES

Many years ago when our older children were young teenagers, our supper hours were not always peaceful meetings. Usually someone in the family had had a bad day at school and was quite willing to cast a black cloud over the supper hour by sharing information about the experience. Before long, the meal deteriorated into a barrage of complaints, arguments, and rude exchanges.

One day I had an idea that resulted in the inauguration of a new game at suppertime. We would begin supper discussions by taking turns talking, and each family member was expected to share *one* positive event that had transpired that day. When everyone had taken his or her turn, we took a second round, and after completing it, the agreement was that the third round could comprise a complaint. I am happy to report that we *never* did a third round. After two rounds of sharing positive thoughts, the atmosphere of the supper hour changed so much that everyone wanted to rejoice in the shared good news.

There were times when one of the children did not feel like participating in "playing positives," but they were not allowed to break with procedure. In my day, we called this parental discipline. By the second round, everyone had warmed to the idea, and in a very short time, our supper hours were again completely transformed.

In 1982 I published a book entitled, *The Helping Book,* (Hamilton, ON: G.R. Welch), and in one chapter outlined the activity of playing positives. A few years later, I received letters from several readers who had initiated the practice at their supper hour for the same reasons. As one reader put it, "You helped change our supper hours from times of turmoil to times of enjoyment."

Based on this feedback, I decided to initiate a similar practice in my university seminars. In a course on multiculturalism in Canada, I gave opportunity for students to share "Meaningful Multicultural Moments" with their peers at the beginning of each class. Each class in a course on Aboriginal education was started with the sharing of "Anecdotes of Aboriginal Awareness." A graduate seminar I offer on religious education begins with items pertaining to "Relevant Religious Reality."

The highlights of playing positives are these; first, when an individual is sharing, no one is allowed to interrupt them. This gives the speaker his or her brief moment "in the sun," so to speak. It affirms the speaker's identity, but also teaches listeners to respect the moment when others are speaking. Second, and most importantly, setting a positive tone for a meeting makes all the difference in the world. It is relatively easy to decide which route to follow—positive or negative. I guarantee the former; try it, and you'll see!

VARYING PERSPECTIVES

Jesus once said, "a prophet is not without honour except in his own town and in his own home" (Matthew 13:57b NIV). A contemporary unnamed prophet put it this way; "The best compliment a person can receive is to be accepted by one's family or home community. Come to think of it, being accepted by one's acquaintances or neighbours isn't such a bad feeling either."

I learned the truth of this principle the hard way.

Huntington Hills Community Church (HHCC), where I served as pastor for 12 years, was an experimental church, quite typical of the sixties. As I have indicated elsewhere in these memoirs, the backgrounds of this unusual congregation could vary a great deal from Sunday to Sunday, but the basic intent was always to worship God while trying to be relevant to the times. Once a month the whole congregation met together for worship and the entire program was geared so that even the youngest child present would get something out of the experience. This was appropriately called, "Family Sunday."

One family Sunday we decided to share aspects of our own family life with the church. Our three oldest children, Bruce, Karen, and Gaylene, were invited to share the platform with me and the plan was that all of us would engage in talk about family procedures at home. It was a foolish and embarrassing plan, and it almost destroyed my ministry. Every subject I approached about family rules from driving habits to staying up late, to doing homework was contradicted by the opinions of at least one of my children.

"Oh, no, Dad," they responded to everything I insisted we did at our house. "That's not the way it is at all. In fact, Dad behaves *this* way!" Then they would go into long diatribes about how they *wished* I would behave. It was a most embarrassing experience and the congregation loved it! Finally, they had their minister where they wanted him. He was being made completely vulnerable.

I am not sure what I learned from this experience, nor what I was *supposed* to learn from it, but I do know this. After that, I mounted the church platform a little more certain of what to expect when I got there. I also tried to listen more carefully to the concerns my children voiced and tried to keep my own behaviour a little more in line with their perspective on things.

Come to think of it, that's not bad advice for any parent.

IMPORTANCE OF EDUCATION

I have always had mixed feelings about my academic capabilities, and my doubts probably originated in grade one when I was assigned the role of "Simple Simon" in the school play! Several years later, when I had nearly completed the fifth grade in Trail, British Columbia, my parents decided to move back to Saskatchewan where they had purchased land with the intent of taking up farming. Now I encountered an entirely different school curriculum than was the case back in Trail and my grades faltered. That same year we moved back to BC for the winter then back to Saskatchewan in time for spring planting. By now, I was in grade six and again had to adjust to a different curriculum just before finishing off the year. When I reached grade seven, we had moved to a new district in Saskatchewan and registered in the Wingard School. Since I was the only student in grade seven at this school the teacher promoted me to grade eight and again my grades suffered.

I am happy today that there were also good times. One of my best memories of this particular school was the way our teacher, Miss Eileen Hagen (from Hagen, Saskatchewan), taught fractions. Miss Hagen would draw a huge pie-shaped circle on the board, divide it into eight pieces, and shade in three of them. She would then move from one student's desk to another, perch herself on the desk and sing out what my brother and I called a four-line ditty, lowering her voice with each line. "How many parts were shaded? How many all together? What fraction is it then, of the parts that were shaded?"

My brother and I took to the ditty and put it to music. Then, when we were milking our farm cows we would sing the ditty, and at the last bar of the ditty, squirt milk into the mouth of our nearby cat who was waiting to be fed! It was a neat way to synthesize what we learned in school with our work responsibilities.

In order to complete high school after grade eight, I enrolled in the Saskatchewan Government Correspondence School. However, having to assist with daily farm chores took time away from my studies so that once again, my grades were nothing to brag about. Each spring I traveled to nearby towns, stayed in boarding houses, and wrote examinations set up by the Saskatchewan Department of Education. My father thought the whole enterprise was a waste of time (partly because of my low grades), but my mother always encouraged me. Dad himself was in the middle of the sixth grade when he was snatched from school and told to help with farm work. A very bright man, who did well in several different businesses, I often wondered what he might have become if he had had the opportunity to stay in school.

My mother's standard line was this; "Stay in school, John," she would say encouragingly. "Then some day you will get a good job, wear a white shirt, and never have to work hard again!" Mother was almost completely right, except for the part about never having to work hard again. I have come to learn that clergymen and professors are almost continually involved in stressful activities that consume time, but I am still very grateful for my mother's encouragement.

When I finally reached graduate school I discovered that the more time one has to devote to one's studies, the more academic rewards one reaps! In graduate school my grades went up significantly and I gained new confidence in my academic abilities. Now I use my early educational experiences to encourage my students to realize that their best years may still be ahead of them.

Rev. John W. Friesen, Ph.D., D.Min., D.R.S.

PROFESSIONAL QUALIFICATIONS

Elsewhere I have detailed the custom of the Silvergrove Church of God (headquartered in Anderson, IN), to involve members of their youth group to participate in various parts of worship on Sunday mornings. During the several years that our family attended that church my brother, David, and I had pretty well handled every item of worship except for preaching. That responsibility was left to the pastor or a visiting evangelist.

On Sundays when it was physically impossible to cross the North Saskatchewan River to attend the Church of God, we opted to visit the local Mennonite Church. One highlight of their overall church program was an occasional Sunday night event—the Christian Endeavor *(Jugenferein*, in Low German)—held every three weeks. At the end of each event, an elected committee assigned various items to representative families, and everyone got very excited about what would be expected of them. The list of items was read out, just before closing prayer, and it consisted of musical items, poems, Scripture reading and prayers, and a brief talk (not a sermon). Gradually, the committee began to assign responsibility for the talk to younger people, and when I was seventeen years of age, I was asked to present such a talk. I was very excited about the privilege, and studied the Bible hard to find just the right thoughts. When the evening in question came, I mounted the pulpit and bravely delivered my thoughts in about ten minutes.

Little did I know that this simple act of mounting the pulpit would force the closure of that church for six months!

During this time, locally elected laymen led many Mennonite churches that could not afford to hire ministers. These individuals were perceived by the congregation to have the gift of interpreting the Word of God. The layman responsible for this particular congregation was not in attendance the evening I gave my talk, but word reached him that I had *stood behind the pulpit* when I spoke. *This*, in his estimation was tantamount to sacrilege. Only duly elected ministers were allowed to stand behind the pulpit. Various committee members tried to explain to their leader that I was probably not aware of this rule because the practice at the Church of God practice was that anyone taking part in leading any part of a worship service could stand behind the pulpit.

The explanation was to no avail, and the elected minister resigned. Thus, the church stood empty for six months; it took that long for church members to talk their leader into returning to his position. After that, my family's presence at the Mennonite Church was scarce. I remember how ashamed my mother was at my behaviour despite my innocence regarding Mennonite pulpit protocol.

Two decades passed, and the district in question decided to have their first ever reunion. A worship service was planned and as part of the program, I was asked to be the speaker. Now an ordained minister, I recall at that reunion meeting the man who had objected to my standing behind his pulpit. It was a brief but friendly meeting. Now, this lay minister was listening in the audience to the very culprit whose innocent actions had motivated the old minister temporarily to curtail his own ministry.

I wondered what he was thinking; I *know* what I was thinking.

A SUPPORTIVE ROLE?

It is always enlightening, but sometimes disappointing, to discover what people really think about one's abilities. While studying at the Mennonite Brethren Bible College (MBBC) in Winnipeg, I became aware of opportunities to participate in college dramas. I discovered that the college sponsored several dramas each year and I was always invited to play a part—without auditioning. Some of the parts I played were that of an African chief, an inebriated husband, and the prince of all evil spirits. The play that included that last role certainly raised some eyebrows in the Winnipeg Mennonite constituency! Some of the leading elders of the local church were uneasy that the devil would be portrayed on a Christian college platform. They voiced their distress to the president and the play's run was cut short.

I thought it somewhat incongruent that though my dramatic roles won public praise, I was never asked to speak in college chapel. Instead, some of the more "holy" types often filled the college pulpit during compulsory chapel services. One day I approached an advisor for whom I had considerable respect and asked why this was so. Why could I play somewhat lauded dramatic roles and never be asked to speak in chapel? He laughed a bit at my query and then "comforted" me with these words.

"Well, that's you, John. That's who you are! You are a dramatist. God can use people in a variety of roles and that is yours. That's who you are! Don't try to be someone else."

I never did figure out exactly what the man meant until a decade later upon completion of a Ph.D. Degree at the University of Kansas. I was teaching summer school at the University of Lethbridge, and while there, I chanced to meet that former MBBC advisor at a church conference. When he enquired as to what I was doing, I told him my scholarly tale. He seemed quite shocked that I had completed a doctorate (something he never attained), and said so. In fact, he said it three times. This was his exact response to my news. "You *got a* Ph.D.? You got a *Ph.D.*? *You* got a Ph.D.?"

I assured him that this was indeed that case and then it suddenly became clear to me what he had meant when he had advised me to participate in dramas at college and not worry about speaking in chapel. He thought I was an entertainer or a clown, and certainly not a preacher or a scholar. Naturally, I was disappointed in his response to my news.

It is always enlightening to discover what people *really* think about your potential, and sometimes you would really rather not know.

GETTING IT RIGHT

Like my student peers in Bethany Bible College, I was young, inexperienced, somewhat uninformed, but quite fervent about presenting the Gospel. This particular college was located in a Mennonite community, and although I should have been more familiar with its operations, my lack of knowledge with its inner workings awarded me with an unusual experience featuring an unusual admixture of ethnicity and Christianity.

It seemed that the local Mennonite Brethren Church was bursting at the seams with an unexpectedly large number of teens and a short supply of Sunday school teachers. The local Sunday school superintendent happened to be acquainted with one of my colleagues, Walter Unger, who was a member of a nearby Mennonite church of the same denomination. The local Sunday school superintendent appealed to him to find someone who would be willing to help teach Sunday school. Being fervent in faith like myself, Walter agreed to take on the task, and asked me to work with him. I was elated. We were assigned to teach 20 junior high aged boys, but in a room that held about a dozen. In our zeal, we immediately arranged to use Bible college facilities for our class, which we divided into two smaller groups. We also found assistant teachers among our peers at school. Then, to avoid any threat of truancy, we used our own automobiles to transport the boys to the college, which was only a few blocks from the church. The superintendent was fully apprised of all of our plans.

In due course, the news reached the church board that Sunday school students were being taught by non-local church members, and that even off campus! It did not matter that my friend, Walter, was a member of the same denomination. I, however, was a member of a non-Mennonite church, and the board would have none of it. The class was immediately assigned to one of our assistant teachers (who insisted he did not really want the responsibility), and Walter and I were invited to serve as assistant teachers. Not wanting to further disturb the puristic religious ethnicity of the congregation, Walter and I promptly declined.

I have often wondered what our students made of it all.

Meaningful Moments in Ministry

II.
INITIAL PASTORAL EXPERIENCES

MY CALL TO PREACH

"Well, my fellow Christians, here is your new pastor." With those words, on December 6, 1960, I formally entered the ministry, unbeknownst to the congregation that they were changing ministers.

It was a tiny Mennonite Brethren Church in rural Kansas, not far from Tabor College where I was a student. The congregation numbered about 35, and was made up of three or four multi-generational families. The pastor of the church was Walter Kleinsasser, a sociology professor at Tabor College. Initially he was enthused by the opportunity to serve the church, having graduated with a Bachelor's degree in religion from Grace Bible Institute in Omaha, Nebraska, and looking for a way to operationalize his theological training. After a few years, however, college teaching began to consume all of Kleinsasser's time and his ministry began to suffer. He met with the church board and asked to be relieved. They agreed, providing that he could locate a substitute. I was it.

Aware of my five years of Bible college education, and now a sociology major working with him as his advisee, Professor Kleinsasser one day asked me if I would be interested in ministering to a church that he was affiliated with. I informed him of my life's objective to be a pastor, but was unsure of how to proceed. Mennonite churches at that time did not have very well spelled out procedures for entering the ministry. Kleinsasser indicated that the small rural church he was serving was looking for a part-time minister since he was about to resign. He asked me if I would be interested in preaching at the church the following Sunday, and I assured him that I would be honoured to do so.

After finishing the sermon, the congregation stood for the final hymn. Then Mr. Kleinsasser offered the Benediction and asked the congregation to remain while he made an important announcement. He began by reminding the congregation that he intended to retire from the ministry. He also reminded them that they had agreed that he could do so provided he first found a replacement. Then he announced, "Well, here is your new pastor, John Friesen."

There was an eerie silence in the stunned congregation. No one, including myself, knew what to say. A few brave individuals came up to me and wished me well as their new pastor. Others cornered Mr. Kleinsasser and demanded to know why he had proceeded the way he had. When the dust had settled, however, I was installed as minister of Steinreich Mennonite Brethren Church, my first pastoral charge.

It was almost a year before conference officials became aware of the ministerial change at the Steinreich Mennonite Brethren Church. Therefore, it was almost a year before I was issued a license to preach, perform marriage ceremonies, or serve the Sacraments.

My monthly salary was $75.00 per month and my responsibilities included being in charge of Sunday morning and evening services, as well as midweek Bible study and prayer meeting. My role also involved home and hospital visitation, attending church council meetings, and participating in interchurch activities with other Mennonite Brethren congregations. Made up of only a few families, the annual church budget at the Steinreich Mennonite Brethren Church barely covered my salary so I took a part-time job as janitor at a local Ford dealership. The garage owner let me work as many hours as I wanted so that by graduation time a year and a half later, I was debt free.

I was very grateful for the janitorial position, because at times, the coffers of the Marion Mennonite Brethren Church, as the church later was called, were emptied out and my pay cheque was late. As the church treasurer, a well-to-do farmer said to me; "Well, if the treasury is empty, I guess we'll have to start giving again!" When I left that pastorate, they owed me a month's salary. They still do!

I served that congregation for two years and helped them relocate from the country to the City of Marion, Kansas, where the church still operates today. When the two years were up at Tabor College, I made my way to Emporia, Kansas, for graduate studies at Emporia State University.

YOU FORGOT THE OFFERING!

I often admire the patience that small country congregations have to extend to young, inexperienced preachers who are sent to them. I am sure that they too frequently have to endure a variety of semi-professional (half-baked) behaviours undertaken by their ministerial protégés. This was certainly the case when I became pastor of Marion Mennonite Brethren Church in Kansas.

A half century ago, the program of studies in Bible colleges was basically Bible studies, including Old and New Testaments, exegesis of various books, biblical archaeology, Hebrew history, and personal witnessing. Although many of the students enrolled in those institutions were headed for ministry, little training was offered in such practical arts as formulating an order of worship, preparing a church bulletin, dealing with a church board, or engaging in home and hospital visitation. I suppose that it was simply assumed that if one was sufficiently familiar with the Word of God, everything else would fall into place.

One of my first faux pas had to do with following the order of worship. After I settled in my first pastoral assignment was quite proud of the fact that I managed to make something that looked like a church bulletin on a "hectograph" (a precedent to the mimeograph, which has in turn been superceded by the photocopier). The bulletin included a formal order of worship.

I did a fine job of following the order of worship until I got to the sermon; then I must have gotten either uneasy or excited so that when I finished my homily, I called on the congregation to stand and join in the closing hymn. After that, I planned to offer a closing prayer and benediction.

The congregation had not yet stood to sing the closing hymn when the 70-year-old Church treasurer called out in a loud ringing voice, "You forgot the offering!"

I quickly called for a change of plans, several members of the congregation who had risen to their feet sat down, and the offering was collected, much to my embarrassment.

After worship, my informal mentor had a straight face when he approached me. "I figured you might want to get paid, so I thought I had better remind you to get the money."

Needless to say, I have never forgotten to announce the offering since.

UNOFFICIAL CHURCH FUNCTIONARIES

A lesson I learned quite early in my ministry has to do with who really runs the church, and it is not necessarily the minister or members of the church board. Every congregation, it seems, is operated principally by a small group of self-appointed functionaries (a sociological term). Sometimes this power broking group consists of only one or two individuals, but their opinions on important church matters are highly valued by most adherents.

I am not sure how these power brokers emerge; perhaps it is because of their wealth, charisma, talent, or historic attachment. Nevertheless, these individuals carry a lot of weight in the local church, and even if they do not sit on a board, they are often consulted about important matters. Often blunt in their assessments, a colleague indicated that he was once greeted at the door of his church after worship with these words from a power broker, "Reverend, you disgust me!" Poor minister; he didn't even know what he had done wrong!

I met a locally influential church functionary at one of my first charges. Although it was not her real name, I will call her Louise. Louise was a tall, striking woman, and always the best dressed in church. I had my suspicions that everyone in church was always interested in seeing what Louise would be wearing when she arrived for the Sunday morning worship service. They were rarely disappointed. Oddly enough, as I grew older and learned a bit about fashion, looking back I would have to say that Louise's appearance was always an intriguing mixture of *Victoria's Secret*, and *Saks Fifth Avenue.*

Her husband, Bill, a kind, humble, ordinary looking, yet a successful Kansas farmer always accompanied Louise. Louise used her appearance as a management tool to great effect; when she spoke, everyone listened, and she always held an important church office. When her oldest daughter got married, Louise arranged to have the wedding take place when I was on vacation. Apparently, that way she could bring in an outside minister with more impressive credentials. Of course making the arrangement without my knowledge was against denominational protocol, and Louise even got permission from the church board at a meeting she called while I was away. Board members knew that Louise's request to have the wedding without the resident minister was irregular, but it was Louise's request, so it was readily granted.

I arrived home the evening of the wedding and was surprised to find the church ablaze with celebration. I quickly discovered the reason for the event and being young, impatient, and more than a little self-righteous, the following week I called a meeting of the church board and asked them to legitimize the meeting they had held in my absence. Sheepishly the poor Kansas farmers agreed to do so, but my war with Louise had just begun. After that, I could not do anything right; she criticized my sermons as trivial and off target, and any idea

I put forth at board meetings was severely scrutinized and questioned.

Our war came to a climax when church elections were held and a new pastor-parish committee was established. Louise, of course, was a member of the new committee, and on Sunday morning when I read the list of names of the members and asked them to stay for a brief meeting after worship, by error, I somehow neglected to read her name. It was an honest mistake, but thinking about it later I concluded that there were probably some Freudian undertones to this omission, I truthfully do not know. Naturally, Louise did not remain for the meeting, so as the event ended I rushed over to her home to apologize, but to no avail. "You made it clear that you did not want me at the meeting," she said, and the war went on despite my pleas for forgiveness.

There is an epitaph to this story (I know I should say epilogue). Some years later when the congregation produced a local history book, every minister who had served the church earned a biography of a page or two. My entry, which consisted of one short sentence, read as follows: "John Friesen, a Mennonite, served two years." Louise was either the editor or the editor-in-influence of the local church history book.

When I was transferred to another congregational charge after this experience, I immediately looked for the local community functionary. Guess what? He (a male, this time) met me at the church door with these words. "I think you'll find, Reverend, that we have a pretty good church here, and if you have any questions about how things work around here, feel free to give me a call." Having learned my lesson with Louise, I can honestly say that I never crossed swords with this "community functionary" in the years I served that church.

I am not exactly sure what that says about me!

BUSY PASTORAL SCHEDULE

When I was a young man, I did not know the meaning of the word "priority." I thought I could handle pretty well anything that came my way, at least in the area of scheduling. Some folks probably think I am still oriented that way, but that is another story.

When I was minister of Camp Creek Evangelical United Brethren (EUB) Church near Atchison, Kansas, I was also a doctoral student at the University of Kansas, which was located 50 miles (80 kilometres) south of the church parsonage where we lived. This meant a commute twice a week, but I did not perceive that as a particularly difficult challenge.

One day an artist friend from our congregation, the late Walter Yost, informed me of a teaching vacancy that had suddenly occurred in the social sciences division at Highland Junior College (now Highland University). Highland University is located 30 miles (48 kilometres) north of Camp Creek EUB Church. About this time, I desperately was short of funds, since tuition and travelling costs were higher than I had expected, and my church salary really was not adequate. After consulting with them, I was happy to discover that the church board did not object to my taking the position at Highland, so long as it did not interfere with my church responsibilities.

At first everything went well, even though I was not as familiar as I wished I were with the various subject matters I was required to instruct. These included American government, European history, introduction to psychology, marriage and family, and introduction to sociology. I had no great difficulty with the latter three subjects, but being a Canadian, I was not excessively familiar with the complexities of American government. I take consolation in the fact that even today most Americans cannot define the role of the Electoral College!

I was doing very well with my various responsibilities, juggling a seemingly impossible schedule, until one morning when I was scheduled to teach an 8 a.m. class on European history at Highland College,

I slept in! I looked at the clock and saw I had twenty minutes to drive a distance that would require a full half hour. This meant that even at excessive speeds, which I was quite used to driving, I probably would still be late for class. I hoped that the students would wait for me.

I dressed hurriedly, skipped breakfast, and took to the road. Surprisingly, I was only a few minutes late and my class was waiting patiently. Perhaps they thought that if they had to get up so early for class they might as well make the best of it.

Somehow, I made my way through the day, and it was only when I was preparing for bed that night, that I discovered that in the morning I had pulled my trousers over my pyjamas. I had worn them all day!

Now *that's* busy!

Later I made the grave mistake of sharing this miscalculated mishap with a "trusted" member of the congregation who promptly threatened to tell the congregation unless I behaved. I lived under this "veiled threat" until the day I moved on to another parish!

SLEEPING SAM

There was an older farmer in one Kansas congregation I served who used to go all night fishing "down by the crick," as he put it. After finding a suitable spot, he would put his fishing line into the water and eventually go to sleep. Whenever he felt the pull of a catfish on the line, he would haul in the catch, in preparation for a tasty noon meal the next day.

My fisherman friend was the late Fritz Fuhrman whose reputation was to go all night fishing on Saturday night when his week's work was finished. Of course he was always in church the next day, but he was not always as alert as most of the other parishioners. Sometimes, in fact, to the embarrassment of his wife, he would nod off in church and on occasion even begin to snore. His wife would nudge him until he woke up.

After serving as minister to the church for several months, Fritz decided to inform me of his fishing habit. By now, we knew each other pretty well, and I was aware that he sometimes fell asleep in church after an all-nighter. He assured me that everything would be quite in order even if he *did* fall asleep.

"Don't worry about it, Reverend," he informed me. "I have fallen asleep on a lot better preachers than you!"

Imagine how relieved I felt when I heard his words of reassurance.

TEA FOR TWO

Many times, it has been said that honesty is the best policy and confession is good for the soul, so here goes.

I have always enjoyed visiting the homes of church parishioners. Home visits provide opportunities for ministers to get to know people. It is certainly not enough to shake hands with people after worship on a Sunday morning and then try to minister effectively to their spiritual needs. People are more relaxed in their homes and often prove to be very good hosts and hostesses. Most of them feel that they should serve refreshments to a visiting minister, and this form of hospitality often provides a more informal atmosphere for the occasion.

There *was* one time when I would have been happy if refreshments had *not* been served. I was given a strange tasting cup of tea (at least according to my preferences), the likes of which I have never encountered since. I tried very hard to enjoy this particular cup of tea, but it was very difficult. Finally, to my joy, the hostess left the room to go into the kitchen, and I quickly poured the tea into a very large pot containing a houseplant! I had read that tea is good for houseplants, so I decided to contribute to the welfare of this particular slice of greenery!

When my hostess returned from the kitchen, she immediately peered into my teacup, noticed it was empty, and despite my kindly protests, promptly poured me another cup. I drank that one under her watchful eye!

Well, now the truth is out; but I can't help but wonder, what would *you* have done?

A GIFT FROM THE MEN OF BONANZA

The sixties comprised a period in television history when western movies literally took over the screen. *Gunsmoke* was the longest running western serial, and can still be viewed on many stations on reruns. *Bonanza,* starring Lorne Greene, was a close second, and featured an unusual scenario with an older man governing three grown sons with an iron rule. These and a host of other similar shows were the order of the day and won the hearts of many fans of all ages. This story is about one of those fans.

Friends and acquaintances who have experienced this kind of human tragedy tell me that when you lose a child you never get over it. I believe them, but there is always a possibility that there are lessons for us to learn when God calls a little one home.

Several decades ago, when I was pastor of the Stull Evangelical United Brethren Church in Kansas, I witnessed the tragic death of a five-year-old boy named Gary Lynch. Gary was stricken with leukemia, a deadly disease that sometimes targets very young children. Gary's family was a spiritually strong unit, and a definite asset to the rural church I was serving at that time. When I first heard the news that Gary had been diagnosed with cancer, I rushed to the hospital wondering what I could say when I arrived there. What was there to say, except to turn the matter over to God in prayer and hope that the family would find some comfort in my friendship and concern.

Over the next few weeks, Gary and I became good friends. I was particularly stunned and impressed by his positive attitude toward his sudden loss of hair, decreasing strength, and rapidly weakening condition. While convalescing, he made friends with all of the hospital staff and word of this unfortunate situation reached the local media. A newspaper reporter visited Gary in hospital and even did a story about him. He asked Gary about his hobbies and discovered that Gary liked to watch television.

"What's your favourite TV show?" the reporter queried.

"Bonanza" Gary replied, beaming with joy.

The national wire system picked up Gary's story and it reached the attention of the *Bonanza* stars. The four main actors in the show responded immediately by sending Gary an autographed photograph of themselves with the *Bonanza* set in the background. That story was also featured in the local paper, and Gary kept the picture centered above his bed where he could look at it all the time. He was so proud of that picture.

The expected day came too soon, and God called his little angel home. Many people from the surrounding neighbourhood attended Gary's funeral. No doubt each of them was touched by the all too brief testimony of a very happy child. In only five years of life, he likely touched more lives in a positive way than many people do in three score and ten!

I wrote the following poem as a tribute to Gary and read it at his funeral. Taking charge of his funeral was one of the most difficult things I have ever had to do.

A BRIEF, SWEET GIFT
BY JOHN W. FRIESEN, WRITTEN IN
HONOUR OF GARY LYNCH

Oh, what glory children bring, When we fully grasp their love,
Theirs is of a higher realm, Signifying that above.
God in mercy to mankind, And to show His depth of grace,

Created children—let them live—on the earth in every place,
There to bright the souls of parents, And to let them daily see,
All the virtues of a child—love, and truth—sincerity.
Another truth is shown today, God to us His jewels doth lend,
When their task on earth is done, Draws them to Himself again.
Thank you God, for this brief gift, We will seek to understand
The message you would have us find,
In this event in which we stand.
We will strive to make *our* lives, Qualified for heaven's joy,
Just as we have witnessed in, The
life of this sweet little boy.

JACOB'S ACRE

Generations ago North American families did most things together, particularly activities that were essential to maintaining the rural way of life. Mutual tasks included planting crops, raising vegetable gardens, gathering firewood, picking berries, and caring for farm livestock. This approach to life also affected church life, as was the case with Jacob's Acre, a plot of land willed to the New Eden Evangelical United Brethren congregation at Corning, Kansas. Subsequently, volunteers farmed the land cooperatively. During the sixties, I served as pastor to the Corning-New Eden charge for one year.

While at Corning, it was my privilege to be part of one of the last Jacob's Acre arrangements in Kansas. The New Eden congregation had title to 80 acres (32 hectares) of good farmland and counted on proceeds from the farm to bolster their church coffers. Unlike the good old days when everyone would harness up their horses and spend hours working the cornfields, farmers now brought modern machinery to the task and finished off the field in a relatively short time. Still, the benefits of working cooperatively on a mutual task were very rewarding.

Everyone found a task to perform and looked forward to mealtime when they could be together and share accounts of times past. Every year a new story originated as someone either made a mistake or excelled at a particular task. In this particular congregation, one man, at that time in his mid-seventies, in his youth earned the name of "shuckin' fool" because he was able to clean the husks off one hundred bushels of corn in less than an hour—by hand! That story lingered in the community's story repertoire for several generations.

There is something extremely precious about working together with one's peers in a non-threatening, productive enterprise, even one as simple as harvesting wheat or corn. While the men planted, sprayed their crops or harvested them, women who provided food for the event enjoyed each other's company as they shared responsibilities and told stories, much like those who participate at an Amish barn-raising.

North America lost something when that rural lifestyle virtually disappeared, but some congregations have worked hard to replace what was lost. Fellowship groups, Bible studies, hobby clubs, and sports events sponsored by churches have to some extent substituted for the fellowship once so much a feature of rural communities. It is even a small comfort to know that in many small rural towns and villages, the same spirit of cooperation and fellowship so much a part of the continent is still alive and well.

As the Old Testament prophet, Amos (3:3 KJV) put it, "Can two walk together unless they be agreed?" We could use a bit more of that kind of consensus these days!

Rev. John W. Friesen, Ph.D., D.Min., D.R.S.

A CONFERENCE DILEMMA

Most church denominations meet for annual conferences as a way to hear reports of progress made, celebrate the lives of those who have gone beyond, and encourage one another. The Evangelical United Brethren denomination in Kansas was no exception in this regard, and alternated the conference site between two church camps located at the cities of Topeka and Salina. Delegates to the conference were chosen by local church members, and the number of individuals a congregation could send depended on the numbers on their membership roll.

One year I traveled several hundred miles to Salina, Kansas, with our local church delegate named Floyd Schroeder. Floyd was a dear, God-fearing farmer with a shy, strong spirit and a heart of gold. He and his family rarely missed a church service, morning or evening, and were always present at midweek Bible studies. I would have considered them among the most loyal church supporters in the community.

When Floyd and I arrived at the Salina camp it was very hot, and the barracks to which we were assigned had no air conditioning. I am sure that this situation did not bother either of us, but what *was* upsetting was the nature of the provided accommodations. The bunk beds on which we were expected to sleep were just a yard (1 meter) apart, and our suitcases were supposed to be stored under the bottom bunk. There did not even seem to be room to dress or undress. The situation was definitely going to be overcrowded and it looked very uninviting. Floyd and I were not relieved by the fact that conference delegates were pouring into the barracks by the dozens.

Without speaking, Floyd and I exchanged glances, but somehow we knew what the other was thinking. It was not hard for a farm-raised pastor and Kansas farmer to be that far apart in their thinking.

Finally, Floyd spoke. "Are you thinking what I'm thinking?" he said with a wry smile.

"Yes," I responded, and without further adieu, verbal or otherwise,

Meaningful Moments in Ministry

we took our suitcases and headed for the nearest low-cost hotel. The price was six dollars apiece for the luxury of privacy, but it was money that neither of us ever regretted spending.

Needless to say, for us at least, the conference went off without a hitch!

PROFESSIONAL JEALOUSY?

Naivety and youth seem to be well bonded, and my own experience certainly bears this out. After I was assigned to my first pastoral charge in the Evangelical United Brethren Church, I discovered that I had a lot to learn about the itinerant system.

The process essentially consisted of ministers being assigned, or reassigned to pastoral charges decided by the conference bishop and superintendents. During the last session of a weeklong conference, everyone gathered in the assembly hall to hear the superintendent read the names of the ministers and the charges to which they were being assigned, or reassigned. Many times, there were surprises as ministers heard that they were being relocated to larger or smaller congregations. These changes usually were based on separate consultations with congregational boards and ministers, but even then, there were often last minute changes.

As the assigning of pulpits began, I found myself sitting next to a seasoned minister whose congregation was in the midst of a building program. I saw an expression of shock on his face as he heard that his new assignment meant a move to a smaller congregation located some 200 miles (322 kilometres) further south. As the reading of names continued it was determined that a certain minister was being assigned to a large city church, but a colleague sitting on my other side was not impressed. Although he was the pastor of a small rural church he indicated to me that the Sunday school enrolment in *his* church was significantly larger that that of the city church just mentioned.

Being both young and naïve, I could not believe that it should make any difference to an itinerant minister where he was assigned nor how many individuals were enrolled in the Sunday school program in his charge.

Clearly, I had a lot to learn about human nature even when disguised in ministerial garb.

BAPTISM SECRET

In one country congregation where I served as minister it was the custom for the pastor to memorize the names of candidates to be baptized. It was then his duty to announce the name of each individual to the congregation as he prepared to baptize that individual. Parents of children did not verbally say the name of the child to be baptized to the minister as the Sacrament was celebrated.

An older minister once shared a secret with me about how he handled this challenge. His secret was in the baptism bowl he used. Although brass in composition, the bowl also had a clear plastic liner into which water was poured. The bottom of the bowl, or anything placed there, clearly could be seen through the plastic container. This ingenious servant of God determined a very clever way to assure that he correctly announced the name of each candidate being baptized.

After recording the names of those to be baptized, this minister typed their names on a slip of paper that he placed under the bowl's liner. Then, as the service progressed, he would dip his hand into the water, read the name of the candidate from the list placed under the liner, and announce it to the congregation. Now there was really no need to memorize the names of the baptism candidates, nor make an error during baptism.

Using this unique approach, I once baptized ten children from the same family in the same service, without their parents repeating their names. I got all the names right, thanks to this ingenious method, and much to the amazement of the congregation. Of course, I had the parents deliver up the children from oldest to youngest so their names would match the descending order of names that I had placed on the bottom of the baptism bowl.

Later it occurred to me that if the parents had not presented the children to me in the right order, there could have been some embarrassing confusion.

SETTLING DISPUTES

After surviving many years of professional ministry, I have come to the conclusion that God *does* work in the church, but often this happens despite our participation in it, not *because* of it!

I have also come to believe that congregations that lack vision are more apt to yield to the temptations of inner conflict than those that are heavily involved in local or foreign mission work or evangelism or even a building project. It seems that the old proverb may have had it right; "Idle hands are the devil's workshop." And, ah yes, the human factor is always involved as well.

A case in point pertains to a disagreement that the members of a little old Western Canadian country congregation had about repainting the trim inside their otherwise white sanctuary. After weeks of deliberation at church council and congregational meetings, it finally came down to choosing either green or blue as the colors for the interior trim. Lengthy further discussions and debates did not bring the matter to a satisfactory resolution, so the "green party" finally took matters into their own hands.

Meeting secretly in church one Saturday night, they brought gallons of green paint and long ladders with them and painted all the trim in the sanctuary to their chosen shade. When they congregation arrived for worship the next morning, they found the sanctuary trim completely redone.

A colleague who reported the story to me did not recall that anyone left the church over the matter.

A similar incident occurred in another rural church within the same general region of the country. This time the dispute had to do with relocating the church building to a major country intersection located five miles (eight kilometres) down a long sloping hill. A segment of the congregation believed that the church could become a more visible and possible effective organization if the church building stood at a more strategic location—at an important community cross roads instead of on a hillside five miles (eight kilometres) from the crossroads.

Once again the discussion went on for several months with no resolution in sight. Then one late Saturday night several determined and ambitious farmers jacked up the church building, put wheels under it, and pulled it down the hill with several teams of horses.

When the congregation arrived for worship the next morning they could not find their church. A little informal research quickly showed them that the church was now located at the bottom of the hill near the much discussed country intersection.

Once again, it was reported that no one left the church over the matter.

MY FIRST CHURCH CONFLICT

Early in my ministry, I arrived at my new charge on a Wednesday night, just as a group of volunteers were practicing for a church play. The practice was not going well, and soon two women began by arguing with one another, then shouting at each other. One of them, no doubt hoping to gain support for her position, stated pointedly, "Why would you talk to me in that tone of voice right in front of our new minister? You've got your nerve!"

Needless to say, I was flabbergasted, and stood speechless, barely keeping in mind a piece of advice I had read some years earlier. An elderly minister once advised his protégé, "When you get into an impossible church situation and you don't know what to do, follow this advice; "Stand in a corner, keep your mouth shut, and smile a lot!" I did just that!

Sadly, I later discovered that one of the families connected to the church promptly moved to another congregation, as a result of that incident without even giving me an opportunity to try to work things out. Sometimes things happen that way, and most ministers would likely feel as I did—that they should have been able to do something about the matter.

PRISON TIME

While attempting to live on the salary of a student minister it was sometimes necessary to find extra employment elsewhere. For this reason, while serving the Stull EUB church, I obtained a part time teaching position at Highland University in Kansas, which was located nearby. I was given the opportunity to instruct night classes at Fort Leavenworth Penitentiary. I was delighted about the assignment, and always willing to function academically in a different sociological milieu. As it turned out, however, I was not exactly prepared for the nuances of prison life. For example, I had to work my way through seven locked gates before I reached my classroom. I also discovered that my students had engaged in quite diverse and illegal activities that led to their incarceration.

My best student was in prison because he had apparently poisoned his wife and then cashed in her insurance policy to obtain funds with which to pay passage for a married woman in England. Somewhere along the line, an investigation ensued, and he got caught. I will say this though; he was certainly an eager sociology student!

Fort Leavenworth Penitentiary had very strict rules about the kinds of courses that could be taught, and the nature of materials such as books, films, or videos that could be brought into the classroom. Usually the warden's assistant on shift examined any teaching supplements I brought in to the prison. In order to comply with the rules, I ended up showing only military movies as course supplements.

My harried lifestyle as pastor, part-time student and part-time teacher, sometimes overwhelmed me. One evening I arrived at Fort Leavenworth Penitentiary to teach my class, looked into my briefcase, and discovered that I had left behind all my notes—including my textbook! I was responsible for a course on American government, something with which I was not too well acquainted as a Canadian. Come to think of it, being educated in Canada also meant that I was not too familiar with Canadian government either. We did not study Canada at school in my day; everything was about happenings in Europe. Still, I studied hard in advance for the course on American government and I was sure my students were learning something of value. Now, without my carefully prepared notes, however, I was virtually unarmed.

Quickly I asked one of my students if I could borrow his textbook for the evening and he graciously complied. I scanned the assigned pages for the evening, adlibbed as much as I could, and desperately tried to engage my students in discussion. The topic that evening was *habeas corpus*, the case of the missing body, and I was greatly relieved to discover that my students knew a great deal more about the subject than I did. We had a lively discussion. There was also the factor in play that if their parole hearing was to occur soon, many students would enrol in several offered courses to make their case look stronger. If their requests for parole were rejected, they would simply drop all courses. Subsequently, one of my courses began with an enrolment of forty, but dropped to less than half of that number after parole hearings were held.

The practice of offering college courses to inmates *can* have positive effect. Sometime after my teaching career at Fort Leavenworth Penitentiary concluded, I was walking from one building to another on the main campus of the University of Kansas, and a man beckoned toward me. He kept his voice down, and it was evident that he wanted to speak with me in secret. He motioned me off the sidewalk toward the back of a building. The invitation seemed innocent enough so I followed him.

"Do you remember me?" he queried. "I was one of your students at Fort Leavenworth Penitentiary. Studying there was one of the best things I have ever done. I transferred my courses to KU and I will graduate in another year. I am so excited and I just had to tell *someone!*"

This was clearly a case of effective prison rehabilitation. This young man got a second chance in life because of someone's efforts to make higher education possible for prison inmates.

I saw a parallel to the young man's experience in the Scriptures: "I tell you that in the same way there will be more rejoicing in heaven over one sinner who repents than over ninety-nine righteous persons who do not need to repent" (Luke 15:7 NIV).

COMMITTED STEWARDSHIP?

Small country churches occasionally have secrets, even though they sometimes try hard to keep them. A church treasurer, for example, is sworn to secrecy, particularly with regard to who might be a generous or stingy giver. In this case, I learned about an event many years after it had transpired, with no names mentioned.

In one church I served, the church treasurer had held office for many years and witnessed many things. The story he shared with me had to do with a special money-raising project that had taken place some years earlier. From time to time, all congregations sponsor special money-raising projects and everyone is invited to participate as they see fit.

In this particular congregation, there was one individual who did not contribute a great deal to ongoing church expenses. In fact, he usually dropped a mere one dollar into the offering plate, despite the fact that he was financially as well off as most people in church. When the congregation voted to buy 50 new chairs for the dining hall, this individual gave the treasurer his usual one-dollar contribution toward the cost of the chairs. However, when it came time to discuss the kind of chairs to purchase, this individual had a great deal to say.

The treasurer, being the only person in the room who knew how much this individual had contributed to the cause, later told me that he was very tempted to give the man back his dollar and ask him to stop talking! Of course, he was committed to maintaining confidentiality, and our "generous" giver was free to continue to express his opinion.

SETTING MINISTERIAL PRIORITIES

Some years ago, a ministerial friend of mine told me how his experience in setting priorities in pastoral ministry had developed.

One evening his wife announced that she and the children decided they wanted to see as family movie with both parents attending. My friend, the busy clergyman, begged off; there was some kind of church committee meeting he had to attend, and, as he told his wife, as much as he would like to be with his family, he simply could not participate. So off his wife and children went to the movie.

In many churches, it is the policy that the minister be considered an ex officio member of every church committee. This means that he or she is invited to attend meeting of any or all committees if he or she wishes, but they will not necessarily be able to vote on matters pertaining to the work of the committee. It was just such a committee meeting that my friend was attending.

As the chairperson moved through the agenda it suddenly became clear to my friend that this was not really where he wanted to be. He would rather be with his family. Quickly he excused himself, left the meeting, and went off to join his family at the movie theatre. He later told me that after that experience he never had difficulty setting priorities for himself.

My own application of this principle is evident in this experience. For many years my wife, Virginia and I occasionally performed weddings for acquaintances that were not members of our congregation. In one instance, we did a wedding for the daughter of an academic colleague of mine. At the wedding reception, we realized that this man, the father of the bride, was the only person either of us knew at the wedding.

To make matters even more interesting, the tables at the reception were arranged to seat only two or four people, and we were placed at a table for two. After a brief discussion, and allusion to my clergy friend's experience described above, we decided that we would rather be at a table for two at home. Quickly we excused ourselves, slipped out of the room, and went home. After that experience, we became very hesitant to perform weddings for mere acquaintances, and when we did perform them, we usually inform them ahead of time that we won't remain for the reception.

We decided that it was a matter of setting priorities.

MY FIRST ALTAR CALL

Prairie evangelism has a history of strong connections to altar calls. Evangelists used to preach the Word, and then ask hearers to respond by "hitting the sawdust trail." Crusades used to be held in huge tents and the center aisle leading toward the altar was lined with sawdust; hence, the term, "hitting the sawdust trail" meant going forward to the altar by way of the center aisle.

My departed brother, David, was always a softhearted fellow and as a youth often responded to altar calls for spiritual rededication and renewal. Sometimes I would try to hold him back because I was embarrassed that he was *again* making his way to the front, but he always brushed me aside. I sometimes wonder if I shouldn't have hit the sawdust trail more often myself!

One evangelist, who visited our congregation each year, offered a free Bible to anyone who responded to his altar call. One young girl in our community annually went to the front to "get a Bible." She said she liked new Bibles!

During my Bible college years, I, like other students, was invited occasionally to preach evangelistic sermons in nearby churches. One northern Manitoba congregation wanted to celebrate Thanksgiving with a series of weekend services, and so invited two of us to come and preach. My colleague, the late Harvey Goosen, being a bit older than I, and more experienced, was to preach in the morning and evening services and I was to look after the afternoon meeting. Both of us looked forward to the experience. Not only was the church located several hours away by automobile travel, but also it was also located in a remote northern fishing village. Harvey and I looked forward to learning about life in such a community, and we were especially proud that they had asked two Bible college students in training to minister for such a special occasion.

The drive up to the village was beautiful because most of the trees still had red, gold, and orange leaves on them. No snow had fallen yet, which was a bit unusual for northern Manitoba in October, and before we knew it, we had reached our destination. We arrived on Saturday night and prepared to participate in three Sunday services and then head back home into the night to be ready for college classes the next morning. The women of the church were ready for the event and billeted us to two families who provided a rich breakfast the next day. We soon discovered that here little time for sightseeing or visiting. We were on duty full-time.

Harvey preached in the morning and I was very impressed with his content and style. At the end of his sermon he gave the classic altar call that we were instructed to give at the end of every sermon we preached. Harvey invited anyone who wished to speak with him to do so after the Benediction. He gave the invitation, but no one responded.

After an unusually heavy noon meal, the congregation headed back into the sanctuary for another theological onslaught, this time from myself. After challenging the now sleepy group, I too gave the expected altar call. For a while, no one headed to the front of the church where I was standing, and the congregation began to leave the sanctuary. After a few minutes had passed, however, an older gentleman approached me. My heart jumped in a mixture of surprise and excitement. Imagine, *my* sermon had been effective! Someone wanted to discuss spiritual matters with me. I recalled that the gentleman had been watching me intently during my delivery, but I was not prepared for the nature of his query. I really was in for a surprise!

"Young man," he said, "I notice that you are wearing very heavy black rimmed glasses (they were in style then). Do you by any chance have a hearing aid in them? I am looking to buy hearing aids, and have heard that they put them into the frames of glasses. I was wondering if you had such a pair."

My heart sank, as I saw my budding career as evangelist sink into the ground. I informed the man that I did *not* have hearing aids in the frames of my glasses, and I watched him walk away looking somewhat disappointed. After that, whenever an individual approaches me in my ministerial capacity, I *never* try to guess what his or her query might be.

By the way, I now *do* wear hearing aids, but they hide secretly away in the inner canal of each ear!

MY VERY BRIEF BASEBALL CAREER

As every minister knows, it is always difficult to follow a successful pastor. When I arrived at the Camp Creek Evangelical United Brethren Church I soon discovered that my predecessor, "Reverend Chuck" (the late Rev. Charles McCullough), was an avid baseball fan—and a very good baseball player. The congregation even sponsored a church team that each week played against other church teams in the area. On arrival, I was immediately invited to play on the team because it was assumed that I would be able to play as well as Reverend Chuck. The team was soon to be disappointed.

I was assigned a position in right field, probably because my abilities in other areas had not yet been proven. The games were played during the evening in a brightly lit baseball field. I was a bit overcome by the whole experience since I had never played any sport under lights. My eyesight wasn't (and isn't) very good either, since I have worn glasses since I was ten years old. In addition, in the farm community in Saskatchewan where I grew up we played all sports—softball, hockey, and volleyball— during the day because there was no electricity. This would be my first experience trying to catch a ball with a glaring light in my face!

The game got underway and by the 7th inning, the score was tied 4 to 4 with the opposing team up to bat. Then the batter hit a fly ball out to right field and I saw it coming down at me, somewhere in the center of the light that was staring me in the face. As I held up my glove to catch the ball, I heard a loud thud behind me as the ball hit the ground amid odious groaning sounds from my colleagues. It was a home run, and so the opposing team won the game. If the team went for coffee after the game, I was not aware of it. In fact, I was never invited to play baseball with them again.

During the next two years that I served the Camp Creek Congregation, I tried to establish my identity in other ways, but my baseball abilities continued to elude me, as they have to this day. One thing I was sure of; if *my* pastoral successor was invited to play on the church's baseball team, it would not take much for him to outshine my talents in that regard.

Meaningful Moments in Ministry

III.
DEFINING MOMENTS IN MINISTRY

A POTPOURRI OF LEARNED LESSONS

Many of us are aware that unwanted advice is usually disregarded. However, there *are* instances when people say things to us that affect the direction of our lives merely because at that time we are ready to hear them. These may not be particularly profound thoughts, but they are things that we are ready to think about at that moment. Here are a few examples.

When I was 15 years old, a neighbour who had observed the behaviour of my brother, David, and myself, for what I would call a minimal amount of time, mentioned to my parents that he saw great potential in David, but he wondered if I would ever amount to anything. When I heard that, I decided to prove him wrong.

While a student at Bethany Bible Institute (now Bethany College), at the end of my first year, the yearbook committee placed this caption under my picture; "Determination is the surest way to succeed." I liked the caption, and decided that if this notation implied that I did not have academic ability, I would certainly achieve my goals by sheer determination. I wonder if I did.

My wife, Virginia's uncle, Alex Letts, has a "defining moment" saying; "They said it couldn't be done; with a smile he went right to it; he tackled the job that couldn't be done, and couldn't do it." *That* certainly hasn't been my experience, so maybe determination *is* the surest way to succeed! My eldest granddaughter, Brittany Friesen likes this quotation; "The best that we can ever become is when we try to be better than we are."

An African American United Methodist bishop (whose name I have forgotten), once said to me, "I am sure that the Christian church is the work of God. No other institution could be so poorly run and still exist. God is surely working in the church." I would like to think that the bishop was joking, but at times I am not sure that he was.

One day I was describing a particularly difficult personal situation to a therapist, and she said to me, "Is this something you *need* in your life?" I decided then and there that I did *not* need that particular millstone, and immediately discarded it. I remember repeating that sentence to a friend who came to me about *his* personal problem and he subsequently went home to break off his engagement with his fiancé!

Some years ago, a couple, both of which were in their second marriage, befriended me. I could not help but notice that whenever they conversed, they always checked out each other's thoughts before taking action on anything. At first, I thought they were overdoing it, and then I realized that this is what spouses *should* always do to show respect for one another's opinions, and thereby engage in open and honest communication—another defining moment.

Believe it or not, I think that academicians are particularly insecure. Perhaps that is why so many of us pursue a Ph.D. degree; we want to be noticed! A colleague who had never earned a doctorate was once approached about it and she explained. "I did my master's degree in Australia where it takes *two* years. In Canada you can earn one in only *one* year, so you see by Canadian standards I really have more than a master's degree."

Many of us have a tendency to take friendships for granted, but that *can* fade. A psychologist friend of mine, the late Dr. Norman Coppin, who had left the City of Calgary for employment elsewhere once wrote me; "John, if we are going to maintain this friendship we are both going to have to put some effort into it." Therefore, we did and I believe we were both the better for it. Unfortunately, our friendship ended some years later when he died of cancer prematurely. Norman was the kind of friend who sometimes disagreed with me about things, and we would have great arguments, but Norman never took any prisoners! In fact, I believe our friendship grew stronger because of our intense discussions. Thanks Norman.

My doctoral advisor at the University of Kansas was the late Dr. Ernest E. Bayles, a professor of Philosophy of Education. Dr. Bayles wrote a number of significant textbooks and delivered many papers at learned conferences. He was respected scholar at the University of Kansas, a former editor for the Harper and Row Publishing Company, and a past-president of the national Philosophy of Education Society.

One day Professor Bayles read to our class a book review someone had penned of one of Dr. Bayles' textbooks. By all standards, it was apparently a very bad book, and the writer of the review even attacked Professor Bayles personally and stated emphatically that this particular book had no redeeming qualities. Bayles' only reaction to the review of this was; "Students, if you ever review a book, think of the time and energy that the writer must have put into its writing. Surely, the undertaking must have meant something to the writer. Try to discover what that message is when you review a book, and mention that in your review. No one goes to all the trouble of writing a book without thinking they have something to share. Find out what it is!"

Over the years, I have published dozens and dozens of book reviews in a variety of journals, and I have *always* kept that advice in mind.

THE EXCITING SIXTIES

Hippies, flower children, sit-ins, love-ins, anti-Vietnam War demonstrations, and protests of various sorts marked the decade of the sixties in North America. The Christian church was also under fire, and questioning groups quickly formed alternative organizations emphasizing charismatic-like features such as those originated by the Jesus People. It was an exciting time to be involved in church life, even though I was almost a generation too late in fully appreciating the impact of the related social movements. By contrast, a decade later when the protests had died down, the church generally fell into a hapless state and assumed a more neutral role in society.

My foray into the interesting decade of the sixties was as pastor of an interfaith Christian church that quickly grew to 300 participants made up of a variety of denominational backgrounds. The congregational format of Huntington Hills Community Church (HHCC) was particularly appealing to married couples of mixed backgrounds where the partners came from different faith backgrounds. Equal to the challenge of developing alternative ways to worship, one would never know what to expect from a Sunday morning worship service. A volunteer worship committee guided the services and regularly sought input from anyone in the congregation who cared to attend their open meetings.

Some of the more radical experiments at HHCC included regular sermon talkbacks that took place each Sunday with coffee and tea service, right after worship. Once a month, Sunday school classes closed down and the church worshipped together as a family. All aspects of worship including the sermon were geared so that youngsters present could understand them. One Sunday the order of church service was completely reversed, beginning with the Benediction, "just so late comers would know what we do at the beginning of the service." The sermon topic was, "Let everything be done decently and in order" (I Corinthians 14:40), to emphasize the importance of order in God's house. When the musical, "Jesus Christ, Superstar," came to town, local radio station personnel came to church and played the piece instead of the regular morning service. Later they interviewed members of the congregation to determine what they thought of it.

One Sunday the order of worship consisted of items identified on slips of paper placed at random in hymnals beforehand. The items included reading from the scriptures, offering a prayer, leading a congregational hymn, and so on. As each congregant opened his or her hymnal, they were invited to fulfill that item if they found one in the hymnal they were holding. If they were too shy to do so, they were encouraged to find a substitute.

Sometimes I miss the sixties. They were interesting and challenging times for the church. Questions were asked whose answers are sometimes taken for granted by the 21st century church. Not all of the questions *had* satisfactory answers. For those we had to trust that God would take care of them.

We need some of those inquiring minds in the church today, but I fear that many of them have left and are seeking answers elsewhere. We need to have them back, lest we fall into spiritual and intellectual limbo.

THE SPOILED BRAT

Urban congregations pose unique challenges, like having spoiled young men or women in the congregation! In one situation, we had the case of the ornery youth whose father was a member of the church board. This spoiled creature knew it, and milked his privileged position to every advantage. He also had a personality problem that could be defined as permanently obnoxious. An ardent member of the church youth group, he rarely missed a meeting because each gathering gave him another opportunity to insult someone or disturb the meeting in some ill-conceived manner.

One evening our group of twelve youth gathered for their weekly meeting. The event usually consisted of a short Bible study and a social activity. For the latter, someone introduced the exercise of saying positive things about one another. Proceeding around the circle in a clockwise direction, each individual was given opportunity to say something positive about every other member of the group. The process worked well until the obnoxious one took his turn. In each case, he managed to make a positive comment, but followed it up with a nasty observation, usually muttered under his breath. Although I cautioned him to stay within the intent of the exercise, he was completely unable to do so. Presumably, that would have made him vulnerable to the group. I often wondered if his bad behaviour said as much about his parents than it did about him.

Another time the youth group decided to sponsor a 30-hour fast to raise money for a nearby orphanage. The event would conclude with an out of town visit to the orphanage. Of course Mr. Obnoxious was unable to starve for so long a time, so he reneged on the experiment. However, he insisted that he be allowed to participate in the field trip to the orphanage. His parents backed him up, of course; he *should* be allowed to participate in the concluding event, so he joined us on the field trip. Once again, he lived up to his true colors, poking "fun" and criticizing everything along the way.

What makes a young man act this way?

DIVORCE COUNSELING

One of the most unusual tasks I have ever been invited to undertake had to do with an unexpected divorce action. I had been counseling an older couple for several weeks, basically about their failure to communicate. The husband complained that his wife insisted that the marriage was over. She declared herself repulsed by her husband and therefore would not even let her husband touch her. She also reported to me that she had found her husband ogling "girly" magazines and that idea was repugnant to her.

Although somewhat complicated by these observations, the situation did not seem insolvable to me and I said so. I suggested that one behaviour might be directly related to another. My approach was to schedule several sessions together and try to get at the root of the problem. The couple seemed to concur with my suggestion, so I was thoroughly shocked at what transpired the next time we met.

The evening I arrived for our next session, I was met at the door by the wife who received me somewhat coldly. Not particularly put out by this reception, I greeted her pleasantly and inquired as to the whereabouts of her husband. Somewhat bluntly, she motioned toward the next room and informed me that he was "in here." Then she abruptly handed me a sheaf of papers and asked me to give them to him.

"What are these?" I inquired. "What am I supposed to be giving him?"

"Those are divorce papers," she pointed out. "If you serve him with them, it will save me twenty dollars in service fees. Then I will be free of him!"

I must admit that I have had some successful counseling encounters, but this was not one of them.

ENCOUNTER WITH A CULT

Being the pastor of a truly interdenominational church, like Huntington Hills Community Church (HHCC), was a unique experience because denominational loyalty played such a small part. On the other hand, one cannot always count on submission to tradition to get one through tough spots. If someone does not like the way things are going, they can simply leave the church. They do not have to face the anguish of walking away from "the church they were baptized in or married in, or the one in which grandma's funeral was held." If the church were a newly-planted work, as HHCC was when I was pastor, the leavers would not be stricken with what might be called "historical nostalgia." They could simply leave with no strings attached.

Interfaith churches are also ripe for the picking in the sense that other groups may try to win adherents over to their cause. This happened many times during my stay at HHCC, and whenever I heard about it, I would try to engage the would-be leavers in conversation about their reasons for leaving. I once invited a couple over to discuss their intended departure and they brought along with them an "elder" from the group they were joining. The group in question was part of a small denomination that holds to rather unorthodox doctrines, downplays theological training and ordination for ministers, disallows musical instruments, and exalts the role of males in church offices, structure and function. The couple informed me that the leaders of this group had given them satisfactory answers to every question they had posed about Christianity!

As we discussed the couple's intentions to leave HHCC, I assured them that we wished only the best for them and hoped they would be happy with their new affiliation. I mentioned that the congregation felt badly about their decision to leave the church since they had been involved in several important activities. "In any event," I stated, "we hope that you will find what you are looking for with this group." The somewhat protective visiting "elder" remarked, "My, that is certainly generous of you," to which I replied, "It is not a generous act at all. We do not "own" this couple, nor are we their guardians. They are free to do as they choose. I only want to assure them of our best wishes."

After I offered a prayer, the three of them left. Several years later, I learned that the couple had left the group and joined a more orthodox evangelical congregation. Shortly thereafter, I received a letter from them expressing regret at leaving our congregation and offering an apology for bringing an unwanted guest (the "elder") into my home. I immediately responded to their letter, thanking them for their thoughtfulness in contacting me. They have remained my friends to this very day.

MY NEARLY GAMBLING CAREER

Church summer camp is always an exciting time. New friendships are formed, individuals get saved and baptized, short-lived romantic relationships are born, and other campers tend to do unusual things. My own camp experience included nearly all of those events, including learning how to swim after I fell off a log raft into a deep part of the lake.

During the years when I was minister of Huntington Hills Community Church a local committee arranged to rent facilities from a neighbouring denomination, and sponsored an annual weekend family camp. It was great fun. We included all of the typical events in the agenda, such as taking turns cooking and cleaning up, engaging in Bible studies and worship services, and having fun times in the nearby shallow river. We even found a deep enough pool at a river bend to be able to hold immersion baptism services for those who requested it.

One evening, however, I came across a group of men playing cards in the camp kitchen. Having been raised according to conservative Mennonite theology and practice, I raised the question about the appropriateness of playing cards at a church sponsored function. The players, it turns out, were equal to the occasion, possibly even waiting for me to voice my concerns.

"Have a seat, Reverend," one of the men suggested. "Let's talk about your problem." I did not perceive my perspective as particularly problematic, but I did sit down next to one of the players. Then, quick as a flash, one of the men threw a handful of cards in front of me and another dropped several dollar bills next to the cards. A third member of the group sprang to his feet holding a flash camera, and took my picture. But God intervened; the flash bulb did not go off and I quickly left the table while the men both groaned and laughed about the situation.

To date there is no record of my short-lived "nearly gambling career!"

Rev. John W. Friesen, Ph.D., D.Min., D.R.S.

A QUARTET SERMON

Pulitzer prize winning novelist, the late Sinclair Lewis, was once asked to address a class at Harvard University (his *Alma Mater*) on the art of writing. His topic was about motivation to write and Lewis proved himself quite equal to the task. He stood at the podium and spoke; "Do you want to write? Go home and write!" Then he collected his honorarium and went home—obviously to write.

Lewis' behaviour may have disappointed the students who came to hear him, but it has many times served as a source of motivation for me. If you *claim* you want to do something, don't just talk about it, get started! Believe it or not, the first sentence in writing a book is the hardest to compose. Lewis' example certainly inspired my actions in the following situation.

Some years ago, friends of mine who were regulars at a local Free Methodist Church, asked if I would fill their pulpit on Sunday mornings since they were without a pastor. I was already serving a church, but being young, eager, and energetic, I agreed to take on the assignment. Since the service at my pastoral charge was quite early, it was agreed that I would arrive at the Free Methodist Church around 11:30 a.m., enter by a side door, and wait for my turn to take charge of the pulpit. A layman would chair the service—leading hymns and prayers and making announcements—until I arrived. There were a few Sundays when my services were not required, because of other pulpit arrangements, and I tried to make careful note of these exceptions on my weekly calendar.

One Sunday I arrived at the Free Methodist Church as usual, made my way to the platform via the side entrance and beheld a Gospel quartet holding forth in harmony of song. I waited for them to stop singing so I could present my sermon, but they did not. In fact, one of their number informed the congregation: "I know we were only supposed to sing a few numbers, but we believe that you probably do not have opportunity to hear a Gospel quartet very often so we are going to continue." Then they did.

By this time I was feeling a little uncomfortable, particularly since I was certain that the quartet members had seen me enter the platform. For the next half hour, I had several worrying thoughts. Had I come on the wrong Sunday? Was my calendar wrong? Was I getting absentminded?"

The quartet stopped singing exactly at noon, the time when the church service was schedule to end. The church board chairman took the microphone and thanked the quartet members for their music, then announced, "Well, we always expect Rev. John Friesen to preach to us at this time, and although it is a little bit late, let's hear what he has to say."

Perhaps Sinclair Lewis' words were ringing in my ears, as I mounted the pulpit so I spoke these words; "I don't know about you folks, but I am hungry, and it seems to me that the only appropriate action after such a good program of music is to pronounce the Benediction and go for lunch!"

The congregation seemed to be in agreement with this suggestion, so I offered a prayer, collected my honorarium, and went home greatly relieved!

A PROMISING PASTOR IN TRAINING

For six years, I had a formal connection to Regis College, a Roman Catholic seminary committed to training priests for the ministry. I served as a member of the Accreditation and Certification Committee of the Canadian Association for Pastoral Education that met twice annually at Regis College. It was here that I encountered a young candidate whom I considered imminently qualified for ministry. Although we spent no more than half an hour together and I have forgotten his name, his impact on me was significant.

While we had coffee together the young would-be priest appeared genuinely interested in having a conversation with me. He asked me all about my family, my hobbies, and my teaching experience. I hardly had time to ask *him* about *his* life, he was so intent on interviewing me. Suddenly, I stopped him and told him I wanted to know something about *his* interests and experiences.

"You will make an excellent pastor," I told that young man. "You made me feel as though you were really interested in me. That is a good trait because people generally like to talk about themselves and you gave me that opportunity."

As a pastor, I do not often have such an opportunity. Most people I worked with or served in my parish weren't too interested in me as a person. They wanted me to listen to them and possibly to pray with them."

My young colleague smiled wryly, and went right on asking me questions. Today I hope he is leading a parish somewhere. No doubt, he will be listening to people, asking them questions, and gently ministering to them. God needs more pastors like that, and so does the church.

Psychologists tell us that people like to hear the sound of their names spoken by someone else. They also like to experience others showing an interest in their activities and interests. The truth of the matter is that *everyone,* including pastors, like to have someone show interest in them as individuals now and then. It would be nice if parishioners realized that a bit more. This young Roman Catholic pastor in training once again emphasized the importance of that truth for me!

THE STONE WAS ROLLED AWAY

It was Easter Sunday, and it was my turn to present the children's feature during the Sunday morning worship service. The church was gloriously decorated with Easter lilies, the choir had sung beautifully, and my next obligation would be to deliver the sermon. Now, however, it seemed only appropriate to relate the biblical account of what happened that first Easter Sunday, and I tried to do so in language the children could understand.

I gathered the youngsters around me at the front of the church and prepared to inject a bit of drama into my presentation. As is the case with most Christian congregations, a larger than usual number of people came to the Easter service, which meant that the group I was addressing was about twice the usual size.

I related how Mary Magdalene first came to the tomb and met the Master. It was only when she heard Jesus' voice that she recognized the voice of the Savior. Next, the disciples, Peter and John arrived, only to discover that the stone that sealed the tomb had been rolled aside. At first, the disciples were shocked, but gradually gathered their nerve and went into the tomb.

I took the story to its ultimate climax. "When the disciples looked in the tomb," I intoned, "what did they find?"

I was not prepared for the extent to which secularism had invaded the church when several children responded to my question in chorus, "They saw the Easter bunny!"

It took a while to refocus the giggling congregation's attention on the biblical answer to the question!

Rev. John W. Friesen, Ph.D., D.Min., D.R.S.

IV.
PRAYER

COMMENTS ON PRAYER

I once read a story about a family who had suffered the loss of a child but kept their faith firm in God. Many people in the congregation where they attended were encouraged by their testimony in the face of adversity. One Sunday after the family had shared their testimony and thanked God for answering their prayers for comfort and consolation, on the way home, a little boy told his father that he too wanted to believe in prayer.

"Well," said his father, "we all believe in prayer, you, know." The boy thought for a moment and then replied, "Yes, Dad, I know we believe in prayer, but not like *that!*"

I wonder what his father thought about that.

I was personally taught to believe in prayer, but when forced up against the realities of life, I found that my faith was very weak. Then God provided a number of valuable experiences that greatly intensified my belief in the power of prayer.

Several years ago, my wife, Virginia, and I were invited to teach a course on prayer at Prairie Bible Institute in Three Hills, Alberta. Although we felt quite unworthy to undertake such a responsibility, we decided to make the most of it, quite convinced that we would probably benefit more from the experience than our students would. In preparing for the course, we visited a Christian second hand bookstore and purchased a few dozen books on prayer for the sum of 50 dollars. This was a great bargain, but the power of prayer does not come from books. We can only be encouraged and blessed by the writings and recommendations of others. As it turned out, the testimonies of our students were also a vital source of knowledge and enrichment.

One of the greatest influences in appreciating the power of prayer came from the members of our own congregation—the Morley United Church on the Stoney Indian Reserve west of Calgary. Living conditions on the reserve are far from ideal; the community has more than its share of substance abuse, broken and/or neglected families, sickness and disease, and economic depression. Some individuals have upsetting stories to tell about their incarceration in residential schools when they were children. These factors led them to believe in prayer—I mean, *really* believe in prayer.

Each Sunday after church, at the request of parishioners, we have prayer meetings, *real* prayer meetings. Three or four elders and the minister will lay hands on the individual making the request, and all will prayer at once, some (like myself) will pray in the English language, but most of them in their native tongue, which is Nakoda Sioux. Requests for prayer are made with such sincerity and childlike faith that I am convinced that I need constantly to grow in appreciation of prayer. I am also convinced that the answers to prayer we witness in that congregation do not occur because of the strength if *my* faith!

Few of us are probably as committed to praying as we should be. We recently toured southern Italy and discovered a monastery where our guide informed us that in days gone by the monks who occupied it spent eight hours a day in prayer. Our month long tour took us to dozens of churches and because of the example of the monks of olden times, we resolved to offer prayers in every church we visited.

Rev. Dr. Richard Dobbins of Emerge Ministries in Akron, Ohio, recommends keeping a prayer log both for reasons of consistency and to discover the faithfulness of God. He also suggests that when Christians are faced with seemingly insurmountable situations that cannot be altered, they pray through the situation and ask God to provide them with a different perspective on the situation.

As you can see, prayer is a vital resource for all believers.

GOD ANSWERS PRAYER

I do not think that students today are necessarily any better off than we were some fifty years ago, despite the fact that they have access to improved financial assistance. There were no student loans available when I was in Bible College and therefore most of us worked our way through school. There may have been a few financially better off youngsters whose parents paid their college costs, but in my experience, these were few in number. Perhaps this was my perception because I had so little to do with those who had ample financial means at their disposal. By contrast, with our situation, many students today graduate with enormous debts, so I am not sure that they are better off.

While living in Winnipeg, Manitoba, a few of my colleagues and myself obtained employment with Display Industries, a sign painting company that paid us one dollar an hour but often offered us unlimited hours of work. If we worked hard, we would emerge in spring with all debts paid, and then search for a more lucrative summer job. While college was in session, we were required to be on call if someone from Display Industries needed help, and sometimes be willing to take an all night shift. I recall that whenever I did this it was exceedingly difficult to concentrate in class the next day.

In addition to regular classes, like many other such institutions, our college often sponsored special events that students were required to attend. Sometimes these events conflicted with available work opportunities so students had to make tough decisions. Should they go to work or attend the event? Often the decision was based on need—how badly did students need additional funds?

One afternoon during college prayer week, a faculty member

caught up with a few of us who were leaving the campus for work. "Gentlemen," he reprimanded us. "How can you go to work during prayer week? Why not engage in the required activities and trust God to supply your needs?"

One of the braver students spoke up. "We *did* trust God, and He supplied jobs for us. Now we are going to do our part in order to fulfill what He has provided."

The faculty member shook his head, obviously doubting that we had made the right decision. Were we indeed obeying God?

I'll leave it for you to decide.

CONTRACT PRAYER

A Bible college professor who believed in Divine miracles, as I do, pointed out that sceptics would counter his belief with this statement: "Miracles are the swaddling clothes of the infant church." This story may help you to make up your mind on the matter.

The Sunday morning worship services had just ended and members of the Morley United Church congregation were greeting one another and sharing insights about the service.

A young man whom I had never seen before approached me, shook my hand and asked if he could have a conversation with me. Judging by the expression on his face I sensed that the matter he wanted to discuss was serious. I replied in the affirmative and ushered him to a quiet corner of the sanctuary. He was quite blunt in the request he made.

"Reverend," he blurted out. "I have a severe problem with drinking. I am an alcoholic. I want you to help me make a contract with God today that I will never take another drink!"

The procedure for making a written contract with God was new to me, but I managed to write up a brief promise of behaviour for this serious young man. I located a blank sheet of paper and wrote the words, "Today, I (name) testify before God, the Heavenly Creator, that from today on, I will never touch another drop of alcohol."

I drew a blank line at the bottom of the page for the young man to sign his name and he did so. Then he handed me the pen.

"Please sign it," he said as he gave back my pen. "I want you to be a witness to my contract with God. Your prayers will help me keep my promise."

I drew another signature line at the bottom of the page and signed my name. The young man folded up the contract we had made and put it in his wallet. We knelt down before God and committed the contract to Him in prayer. The Lord God was now our third partner. Grinning with joy, my new acquaintance shook hands with me, thanked me, and left the church.

Seven years went by, and one morning the same young man approached me after the Sunday worship service. "Do you recognize me?" he inquired in a friendly voice. I thought hard, but could not say that I did. Seven years is a long time for an aging pastor to recall events. He quickly helped me out.

"I have come to ask you to perform a marriage ceremony for my fiancé and myself," he offered. "By the way," he continued as he removed a worn piece of paper from his wallet, "this is the contract that you and I wrote with God seven years ago. It was about my alcoholism. I have never taken a drink since we made that contract. Thank you for your prayers!"

I cannot recall exactly how I expressed my joy at this occasion, but I remember that we hugged one another amid tears of joy and thankfulness. Then we made plans for his upcoming wedding!

PARADOXICAL USE OF PRAYER

One summer I obtained employment at a lumberyard. I was assigned the task of loading and unloading lumber from railroad freight cars, and even delivering lumber to many different locations in the city by truck. It was hard work, but the good news was that the lumberyard owner said I could work as many hours as I wanted. After putting in 44 hours in a week, my wages of $1.10 an hour went up by fifty percent. I usually managed to put in the required number of hours by the middle of the week so that by Wednesday night I was being paid overtime. During that summer, I made enough money to be able to study for a whole semester without holding at least a part-time job. That experience was unusual, as it is the only time in my life that I have been able to enjoy studying without also holding a job.

The man who owned the lumberyard was a professing Christian, as were many of his employees. Each Monday morning the owner would gather all of the office staff and outside workers in the salesroom and ask them to bow their heads in prayer for the week ahead. I thought that the man's prayer itself was always appropriate to the occasion. In his prayer, he would thank God for His blessings, His provisions, and the opportunity to be able to work. He would ask for safety for the workers, and good health for everyone connected to the business. When the prayer concluded, we all headed out to do our jobs.

One Monday morning after prayer one group of yard workers was a little slower than usual in getting started. When the owner saw this, he roared out; "Come on now men, time is a-wasting. Do you know that it is costing me several hundred dollars an hour to employ all of you? I will lose a lot of money if you don't get to work right away!"

Somehow, I had difficulty reconciling the tone of that lament with the mood of the prayer I had heard just a few minutes earlier.

A NEW MAKE OF LAWNMOWER

The strong faith of Morley United Church congregants clearly influenced our own attitude toward prayer with the result that we now believe more strongly in prayer. Proverbs 3:6 (ESV) reads: "In *all* your ways acknowledge Him, and He will make straight your paths." I have for a long time believed that any topic, no matter how seemingly insignificant, can be presented to God in petition.

One particular Sunday morning, as our worship service was about to begin, I stood at the pulpit and glanced out of the window that was lit up with glorious sunshine. It was a beautiful day; then I noticed that the church lawn had not been trimmed for several weeks and to me it was looking quite unkempt. It occurred to me that this was not necessarily a grave matter of concern to our congregants, but to me a nicer-looking lawn was relatively important. Coming from a background, where appearances are quite often a priority, I reasoned that God's house (and lawn) should always look nice.

I had not really committed the matter to prayer, but God sensed my discomfort and provided a solution. Still looking out of the window from the pulpit, I noticed that three stray horses and two cows had made their way to the church lawn and began grazing on the lawn. I surmised that together the five animals constituted God's lawn mower, and it wasn't long before their work was done and they moved on to greener pastures!

I smiled to myself, wondering if my fellow parishioners, who were quite used to encountering stray animals on the reserve, would appreciate this particular example of God's work.

THE RIGHT PLACE AT THE RIGHT TIME

Proverbs 25:11 (KJV) states, "A word fitly spoken is like apples of gold in pictures of silver." The impact of this verse is that uttered appropriate thoughts can sometimes serve as enlightening moments. In other words, hearing just the right words at just the right time can make a significant difference to one's life! Some people call these defining moments. Here are a few examples.

To this day, on the first day of each university class, I have made it a practice to inform my students that I am a Christian. I have kept up this practice since the very beginning of my 47-year teaching career, even though I work in a secular institution. I do this as a way of cautioning my students to "be aware of where I'm coming from," so they will not unwittingly be influenced in a given direction. Universities, after all, are supposed to be value free institutions, although I believe they are not. In fact, it is my opinion that many university professors deliberately try to influence students to think in a particular way, and they offer no apology for doing so. There are even professors who belittle the opinions of students who are faithful believers in matters of faith, even to the point of making fun of them in class.

In any event, not all of us are so opinioned. One student, a science major who took several of my courses, informed me a year or so later that he felt sorry for me when I stated in class that I was a Christian. As he put it, "Based on my previous experience, I didn't think anyone could teach a course in philosophy and still maintain some semblance of the Christian faith. Now I think otherwise."

One day the dean of the faculty called me in and showed me a letter from a former student who claimed to have contemplated suicide during her course of studies. She stated that if it had not been for my testimony and that of a Christian colleague, she said she surely would have gone through with it.

Another time I received an anonymous note under my office door that stated; "Before the term began I prayed to God that He would send me at least one Christian professor this term, and He did. It was you. If God had not answered my prayer, I was determined to drop out of university. When you announced on the first day of class that you were a Christian, I nearly shouted for joy! God answered my prayer!"

A decade rolled by, and one day while visiting a friend in the country, I had opportunity to meet that particular student. Now a qualified and experienced teacher, she came to my friend's home to thank me in person for sharing my testimony in class. Her subsequent studies led her to assume a teaching career through which she herself could witness, however briefly, to other students.

God works in mysterious ways, His wonders to perform!

A GRATEFUL RECIPIENT OF PRAYER

It is expected that members of the clergy will always be ready to offer to pray for others—at hospitals, in home visits, or by special request, but it is quite unusual for individuals to offer prayers for members of the ministerial profession. No doubt, many parishioners include the name of the local pastor on their family prayer list, but this is not quite the same as someone uttering the words, "May I offer a prayer for you?"

This was my experience at a family reunion several years back. The reunion took place in the province of Saskatchewan, a seven-hour drive from our home. I had been asked to take charge of the Sunday morning worship at the reunion, and I felt quite honoured to have been asked to do so. It isn't often that one is asked to preach to dozens of one's cousins.

My wife and I arrived a few hours earlier than our five grown children did, and we were looking forward to seeing them. They live in different parts of the world now, including British Columbia, Florida, and Ontario, as well as Calgary, so our immediate family reunions are quite infrequent.

It was late Friday evening when we arrived at the scheduled location for the family reunion, and although we do not usually dine late in the evening, we were so hungry that we ventured into a local eatery for a quick meal. It was a mistake I would later regret; shortly after midnight, I developed a very bad case of food poisoning, and my stomach was in utter turmoil for the rest of the night. During intermittent moments when the pain subsided a bit I wondered how I would be able to fulfill my preaching assignment. As the pain continued, I could not take part in any scheduled activities the next day; I was virtually attached to my bed. The fever I suffered lingered on through the night and all through the next day. As Saturday evening approached and turned into night, I felt no better.

It was then that our youngest daughter, Beth Anne, took action. She and her husband, Jason, believe strongly in prayer. Late Saturday night Beth Anne came to my bedside, and her greeting took me a bit off guard.

"Dad," she said, "I know you have to preach tomorrow, and you will need to have your health back. May I pray over you?"

Tears of gratitude welled up in my eyes as I realized that it was my turn to be the recipient of spiritual concern. My daughter placed her hands on me and offered a brief prayer. Being fully aware of her great faith in healing, I placed great confidence in her actions, and soon fell asleep.

I am happy to report that the family reunion worship service went off very well. The guest preacher was in fine form, thanks in part to a kind heavenly Father and the preacher's own daughter!

Meaningful Moments in Ministry

V.
LOVE AND MARRIAGE

DETAILS, DETAILS

The original inhabitants of North America maintained a unique philosophy of life, before European contact, much of which has been changed or even lost. Traditionally, the North American First Nations believed strongly in living in harmony with nature, respecting the interconnectedness of all living things, sharing with the needy, and honouring family ties—including the extended family. Although they had a healthy respect for the past, they did not make many future plans because they believed that the only time that is assured is the present. We have really learned to appreciate this perspective during our twenty-five year stint with the Morley United Church on the Stoney Indian Reserve. We discovered that many deep-rooted Indian values, such as respect for the past and living in the present, are alive and well.

Although church services at Morley United Church are scheduled for 11:00 a.m., they rarely start on time, so we sing hymns until "enough" people get there. We define "enough" to mean at least a handful of people. One Sunday, it seemed that no one was coming to church, so at 11:45 a.m., my wife and I began to pack up our things. Then, a few minutes later, as though they had planned it, all at once 40 people walked in, ready to sing hymns, listen to a sermon, and worship the Lord.

Weddings and funerals are quite another thing, and again, these events rarely start on the scheduled time. When they *do* get underway, funerals can last up to eight hours, including graveside services, preceded by a long church service and a three or four day wake. After the graveside service is over, everyone goes for supper at the home of the deceased's family.

When we first began our ministry at Morley United Church I scheduled wedding rehearsals, since this seemed to be a community custom. I soon discovered, however, that rehearsals were not taken seriously; they were primarily an opportunity for the families of the wedding partners to get together. At one particular rehearsal it turned out that the bride did not show up, neither did her parents, nor the best man, nor the bridesmaid, nor the flower girl. In order to get things underway, it was suggested that we have people stand in for the various positions, and this was what transpired. The next day at the wedding, all of the parties except for the best man, showed up and the wedding went off fairly much as planned.

After delaying the ceremony for an hour waiting for the best man to arrive, who it was learned later had gone into town to rent a pair of nice shoes; the event began with a substitute best man wearing a blue suit. The other attendants were all in black. By the time, the reception started, the original best man showed up wearing a pair of "nice shoes," and he was given the honour of posing with the wedding party for photographs.

Gradually, I learned to understand and appreciate the concept of "Indian time," as it is sometimes called. It does not mean that there is virtue in being late or not showing up, but rather that time is relative to need. If there is an important family matter to resolve, or anything that requires urgent attention, obligations are informally rated and fulfilled in order of priority. Family responsibilities are always given priority and attended to above those related to employment, schooling or business.

There is something fundamentally biblical about this approach. When St. Paul wrote to young Timothy he reminded him, "Anyone who does not provide for their relatives, and especially for their own household, has denied the faith and is worse than an unbeliever" (I Timothy 5:8 NIV).

I sometimes wonder if that commandment still has application today.

IMPROMPTU ACT

Like her mother, our daughter, Beth Anne, believes in the slogan—"waste not, want not." Someone once gave her a bottle of genuine vanilla, not the fake, watered down kind you buy at the supermarket. As everyone knows, a bottle of vanilla lasts a long time, and Beth Anne could hardly wait for the day when the imitation vanilla bottle would be emptied. Then she could use the real thing.

One day her brother, David, came to visit her and among other things, she told him about her waiting bottle of *real* vanilla. David was amused that his sister would wait for such a long time to use the treasured product. To her surprise he took the imitation bottle of vanilla, dumped its remaining contents into the sink, and then announced; "There, now you can use the real thing!"

Comedienne Carol Burnett used to perform such unexpected and unorthodox acts on television. Such actions constitute a rich source for humour, and Carol and her cohorts certainly knew how to make the most of such situations. Perhaps the closest I came to performing a Carol Burnett-like act was at the conclusion of a wedding when I informed an unusually shy groom, "Now, you may kiss the bride."

The groom seemed to hesitate, so gesturing toward his attendants I intoned, "If you *aren't* interested, I am sure that one of these young men may help you out!"

The groom quickly kissed the bride amid boisterous laughter from the congregation.

TRUE LOVE

My first serious introduction to the meaning of marriage came at the age of 16 at the Silvergrove Church of God (headquartered in Anderson, Indiana), when Ida, our youth leader was to be married to her beau, Larry. It was to be an early spring wedding, perhaps a bit too early, because the dirt country roads in our region of the northern Canadian prairies were still covered with bits of ice and snow and plenty of mud. The latter wrought real havoc on the roads whenever our family tried to get to church. Even after our Model A Ford car had maneuvered down the dubious mud-coated river hill road to reach the ferryboat on the North Saskatchewan River, we still had four miles (six kilometres) of muddy ruts to conquer after a half hour ferry ride.

The wedding was set for 2 p.m., and as eager country folks were accustomed to do, we all arrived early. The women and girls were no doubt eager to see what the bride was wearing, and the unmarried youth were eager to see what the unattached girls were wearing. For many young men such an opportunity could perhaps turn out to be a match made in heaven—at least so they hoped!

At the set time, everyone sat on pins and needles, waiting to see the bride, when the minister suddenly announced that the groom would be a little late. He had not yet arrived. The minister suggested that the congregation engage in a hymn sing as they waited. He was sure the groom would be along very shortly. Naturally, everyone was anxious to learn what how the bride was taking the news, but she was safely tucked away in the minister's house where his wife was providing sympathetic support. According to members of the bridal party who had checked with the bride, if she was even a little bit upset, she never let on.

After an hour-long hymn sing and still no groom, the minister suggested that members of the congregation take a break and perhaps get some air or visit with one another. He then proceeded to tour the congregation taking time to speak with everyone present.

Another hour passed, and then two more; still no groom. Of course, there were few telephones in those days, and no cell phones, and certainly, the church could not afford such luxury if it *had* been available. There was simply no way to find out where the groom could be. No doubt, the keepers of reception supplies were also getting a bit worried. Country cooks without microwave ovens can keep meals hot only so long. Once again, all eyes were on members of the bridal party who by now had been assigned the duty of regularly reporting on the bride's reaction to the malaise.

Shortly after the four-hour siege, someone suddenly spotted the groom's car slowly making its way down the road to the church from a westerly direction. Shouts of surprise, relief, and joy echoed through the halls of the little church, and everyone scurried to their places to prepare for the ceremony. Even the minister looked more than a little relieved, but when the bride appeared, she simply looked calm and beautiful. She knew her beloved would arrive. He did—after having to repair a flat tire on his car as well as trying to free his car from a muddy sinkhole! By the way, his wedding outfit showed the results of his harrowing experience, but this did not diminish the happy spirit of the occasion in any way.

Ida and Larry remained happily married for many years until the relationship ended by his departure from the earth to his heavenly reward. Ida's faith in the relationship on their wedding day and the quality and longevity of their marriage firmly planted a positive image in my youthful mind.

MARRIAGE IS A SERIOUS BUSINESS

When I was an upstart and eager preacher, I perceived myself as somewhat of a "Marrying Sam," and thought it my duty to preside at weddings whenever I was asked to do so. Sometimes I performed wedding ceremonies for people I hardly knew. One evening a couple came to my office for premarital counseling, and after exchanging pleasantries, I began to ask more personal questions such as, "Have either of you ever been married before?"

"Oh, I was," the bride-to-be blurted out, "but only for a brief time and I got over it real quick!" Her quick dismissal of the event stirred my youthful pastoral curiosity.

"How does one quickly get over such an important commitment?" I queried, and in response, the prospective bride burst into tears, accompanied by convulsive sobs. When it appeared that she would be unable to regain her composure, her fiancé suggested that they cut the visit short and arranged to come back another time.

I never saw them again!

MINISTER FOR HIRE?

One evening I received a call from a woman who informed me that she casting about for a minister who could "conduct a respectable wedding."

"My daughter is getting married," she ventured, "And since we are not church connected I am phoning around to find someone to undertake that responsibility. I heard that you conduct a pretty good wedding, so I was wondering if you would be available on this particular date." She then informed me as to the day and time of the planned event.

At that point, something unusual happened; my pastoral hackles suddenly heightened.

"I must mention," I began, "that I am really not interested in conducting a 'pretty good wedding,' as you put it. I am more interested in the extent of readiness that the young couple is exhibiting. I would have to meet with them before I make a commitment to officiate at their wedding."

I would have continued, but the caller suddenly ended the

conversation; my telephone unexpectedly made a loud "click." I must have said something wrong.

After that experience, it occurred to me that I would not conduct any more what I call "Yellow Pages Weddings," as I call them. Such invitations occur when someone looks up your name in the yellow pages of the telephone directory to check out your professional aptitude!

Suddenly, I was no longer a "Marrying Sam!"

Wedding vows *are* sacred, and they are not usually said with any measure of ease. Sometimes when I prepare to state the vows for a young couple, I ask married couples in the congregation to hold hands and mouth the words to one another—sort of a renewal of their own commitment. I tell the couple to be married that I am doing this to lighten up what I perceive to be a very serious occasion. In fact, I have seen both (or either) brides *and* grooms shed tears while saying their vows.

Generally, there is quiet shuffling in the congregation after my suggestion has been voiced—no doubt some handholding is happening, but some married couples sit stoically, without even looking at one another. A friend of mine suggested that when this happens, I should ask the bridal couple to look around to witness what they do not want their marriage to become.

Marriage vows are sacred. The ceremony in the *Book of Order* that I use states in part, "No other ties are more tender, no other vows are more sacred than those you now assume. I entreat you both to seek the help of God in this sacred moment, and to look to him steadfastly for his love and grace which will make your marriage rich in comfort and fruitful in service."

CAREFUL PLANNING

One of the weddings I conducted at the Stull Evangelical United Brethren Church was planned to be a real classy happening. Even the rehearsal went off like a Hollywood affair except that the bride made one most unfortunate error. The flower girl she chose happened to be her niece, but she was only four years old. It is always hard to predict what a four-year-old will do at any given moment, particularly when they are called on to perform before a strange audience. I had my doubts about the little girl's performance, and I was surprised how well the she behaved at the rehearsal. She wore a very beautiful dress and made the walk down the aisle with great dignity.

The next day was something else. When the cute little flower girl entered the sanctuary just before the bride, she took one look at the congregation (who were not in attendance the night before), and broke into an ear-splitting shriek, the likes of which could have brought Lazarus out of his tomb! There was *no* way she was going down the aisle, and she did not! Needless to say, the bride was severely disappointed, but we finally got the wedding ceremony underway minus the flower girl.

SOLEMNITY EXCLUDED

As I began to document this incident, I was reminded of another wedding I once conducted that had a unique element of humour about it. As part of their commitment to the Christian faith, and to lend a special context of worship to the marriage, the couple decided to kneel at the altar for the final prayer of the ceremony. As they knelt for prayer, I could hear the sounds of muffled laughter coming from the congregation. I proceeded to offer a prayer for the couple, but it took a few minutes for the laughter to subside. I later discovered that some mischievous friends of the groom had fixated the word "help" on the bottom of each of his shoes. As the couple knelt, the congregation saw the word "help" written on the groom's shoes, and found it very difficult to assume a ceremonial stance!

LET'S GET MARRIED—NOW!

Scheduling events on the Stoney (Nakoda Sioux) Reserve is not always an easy task, basically because the people do not prefer to live their lives by watching the clock or bowing in obeisance to the twelve month calendar. As a result, there are often surprises one encounters in working with the community. Each day is new unto itself, and as a minister to the local congregation, one must learn to go with the flow.

One Sunday morning after the worship service had concluded, an older couple approached me about getting married and I agreed to honour their request. I assumed that they meant that a wedding would be held sometime in the future, but soon learned that they wanted to be married on the spot. They came prepared with a marriage license and a friend who volunteered to serve as a witness.

I was completely taken off guard, of course, since I did not usually carry my "marrying book" with me. I believe the United Methodists call it the *Discipline,* while other denominations call it the *Book of Order.* The couple was quite insistent about getting married, and I was willing to consider doing the ceremony by heart. Now another problem loomed, however, because the Province of Alberta requires that there be *two* witnesses to a marriage ceremony. By now all of the people who had attended the worship service had vacated the church. My wife, Virginia, agreed to serve as a second witness, but she was also asked to serve as pianist for the event. The couple requested that they be able make their entrance into the sanctuary accompanied by the music of the traditional wedding march—followed by their one witness. It was all very interesting.

As I began to recite the wedding ceremony by heart, I was amazed at how much of it I had committed to memory through the years. In fact, I hardly stumbled at all, and the wedding concluded with signing the register. Then the couple posed for pictures—using our camera. Fortunately, we often carry a camera with us so we could accommodate them.

Rev. John W. Friesen, Ph.D., D.Min., D.R.S.

This was not the end of the event.

Several weeks went by and I received a call from the provincial Department of Statistics indicating that the marriage registration I had sent in on behalf of the couple might not be accurate. It had to do with the recording of the groom's name. Would I please get in touch with the couple and verify if the man's name ended with "Jr" as he had indicated to me. The request of provincial authorities seemed quite challenging, since the couple were not regular church attendees. As I soon discovered, by consulting with several church members, they lived a long distance from the church and they had no telephone. Several weeks went by, and I decided I should try to visit this couple and hoped they would be home when I called. I was also just a bit nervous about satisfying government requirements pertaining to the marriage.

The problem suddenly resolved itself—Stoney style! One Sunday morning after worship, the groom suddenly showed up at church and sought me out.

"I heard you were looking for me," he said. "What can I do for you?" I was pleasantly surprised to see him, and said so. How did he know I wanted to speak with him? "Oh, that's the reliability of Indian moccasin telegraph," he said, matter of factly. "Word always gets around the community when you want it to. Just tell someone about it and sooner or later you will get the information across."

We soon settled the matter of the item in question, I telephoned the Department of Vital Statistics to satisfy their query, and the Stoney First Nation made a believer out of me in the efficacy of the Indian Moccasin Telegraph!

A MOUNTAINTOP WEDDING

"Let's walk around until it feels right," the bride said to the groom, and off they went. It was the late sixties. The couple was part of a small wedding party who had just hiked up a mountain after driving their cars up the slope as far as they were able.

Having worked with the groom for several months on a language project with the Stoney (Nakoda Sioux) First Nation west of Calgary, I became aware that he had been in a common law relationship for seven years.

"Why don't you make an honest woman out of your mate?" I asked one day, "thinking that the couple should be ready for marriage after such a long courtship. The soon-to-be groom said he would think about it, and the very next day he announced that there would be a wedding and would I care to officiate.

I was quite surprised by the quick turn of events, and I could only imagine how the prospective bride must have felt when he offered his proposal the previous night! Sometimes things have a way of working out quickly. I agreed to conduct the ceremony, but was quite unprepared as to its format. Normally couples would meet with me for counsel prior to their wedding, and I would offer suggestions as to location, format, and reception. This couple did everything on their own—except for the counseling sessions, of course.

I was informed that the wedding was to be held at the top of a mountain, and a small group of friends would accompany us, first on a car ride up a narrow rock-laden road, and then on a hike to the top. In true hippie style, the groom wore a white smock, derived from an eastern cultural source, blue jeans, and long flowing hair with a ribbon in it. The bride also had long hair and wore a long blue jean skirt with a white blouse.

As the group neared the top of the mountain the accompanying party was asked to remain while the couple searched for "the right place" to be married. A shout from the groom alerted the wedding party that the ideal spot had been located and soon the ceremony was underway. Although I remained true to the Methodist type ceremony I was used to by now, when the vows had been said, everyone was asked to contribute their thoughts. Several individuals cited poetry, someone read from *The Prophet* (very common in the sixties), and others shared "beautiful thoughts. When this part of the process was over, the group migrated back to where the cars were located and shared a bag lunch prepared previously by the bride.

To highlight the event, the groom turned up the eight track tape player on his old Volkswagen bug and everyone danced in the deep grass to Hungarian music.

I recently met again with this couple only to discover that they have been married for thirty happy years. They live in a log cabin in the country in true 1960s hippie style. They have minimal material possessions and although they have use of electric power, their home is not equipped with running water.

The sixties were interesting times in North America. Young people were protesting the Vietnam War, Black Power, representing dissent in the African American community, was in the news, and the hippie movement flourished. Every major societal institution, including the church, was under scrutiny, and change of all kinds was evident. This mountain top wedding was typical of the manner in which North American youth initiated alternative ways to celebrating scared ceremonies.

Who is to say that they did not invent a more meaningful alternative way?

A TRULY INTERFAITH WEDDING

The ecumenical movement of the sixties inspired a series of cooperative movements among churches of different backgrounds and my experience was no exception in this regard. I can remember meeting with couples of different Christian affiliations wanting to have ministers representing both backgrounds to participate in their marriage ceremony, only to be met with resistance from either denomination. My experience with Father Jollie of the Roman Catholic faith was quite different.

In this instance, the bride and groom were both quite devoted to their particular denominations, one toward the Roman Catholic Church and the other an avowed Protestant. I, as a friend of the family, represented the latter affiliation, and was a bit uncertain about working with a Roman Catholic priest. I had previously been turned down when making such a suggestion to another clergyman of Catholic affiliation, so I was not exactly sure how things would turn out. I was quite prepared to cooperate in whatever way I could but I was not prepared for Father Jollie's receptiveness.

The wedding rehearsal went well, each of us agreeing to take turns with various parts of the ceremony. "Do whatever you like," Father Jollie informed me, "As long as I have opportunity to bless the rings we can consider this a valid Catholic wedding. Is that O.K. with you?" I was quite satisfied with this arrangement and almost had to beg my colleague to take an equal part in the event.

The next day, the two of us alternated in performing parts of the ceremony, making certain that Father Jollie was responsible for the ring ceremony at the appropriate time. As the ceremony flowed, at one point it was time for prayer so Father Jollie turned to me, winked, nudged me, and in a low voice said, "You do this one."

Now aware of his unique sense of humour I turned to him and whispered, "No, you do it. This is not what we agreed on yesterday!" Grinning wickedly, he offered a prayer and the ceremony went on.

If all priests were like Father Jollie, I could seriously consider becoming a Christian of the Roman Catholic persuasion!

A DIFFERENT INTERFAITH WEDDING

One day a student at the University of Calgary, who had taken several courses with me, asked me if I would preside at her wedding. It seems that she and her fiancé had consulted the pastor at her church about getting married, but he had refused to conduct the ceremony.

Apparently, he objected to the fact that this woman's fiancé belonged to a denomination of which the pastor did not approve. Since the woman and her parents had been faithful members of the church for many years, however, he did allow her have the wedding in her home church with another minister conducting the ceremony. It was for this reason that the bride-to-be consulted me.

I had previously discussed course material with this particular student, and was impressed with her sincerity. I was aware that she was very serious about her Christian faith and she assured me that her fiancé was too. I met with the couple, and after several sessions became convinced that despite their denominational differences, the couple shared a common faith in Jesus Christ. Their plea, along with my rather cavalier attitude toward denominational differences, made it seem quite logical for me to preside at their wedding.

The wedding rehearsal proved to be a friendly affair as the families of the bride and groom became acquainted with one another. The various members of the wedding party seemed to be very supportive of the wedding couple, and afterward they all met for a rehearsal supper. Things seemed to be going well.

On the day of the wedding, as is my custom, I checked to see that all members of the wedding party were present, then spent the rest of my time with the men. As I arrived at the room where the groom and his attendants were waiting, an unsettled groom confronted me.

"He's out there, "he stammered. "I don't see how he had the nerve to attend my wedding!"

"Who is out there?" I inquired. "Why are you so upset?"

"The minister," he replied, "The one who refused to marry us. He is sitting right out there. Why is he even here?"

I tried to calm down the groom by pointing out that the man in question *was* the minister of the church and that gave him a right to be there, "Just wait until I get started," I assured him. "I will look after everything and you will have nothing to worry about. Try to stay calm and trust me."

The wedding party made their entrance into the sanctuary and I began the event with the expected invocation, "In the name of God, the Father, the Son, and the Holy Spirit." Then I made introductory comments about the couple and emphasized how their love for each other made it possible for them to overcome what might seem to onlookers as insurmountable denominational differences. "They could serve as a model for the rest of us," I told the congregation. By now the groom was beaming.

I have maintained a friendship with the couple in question for more than thirty years and they as a couple have continued to function as a good example of the fact that a strong human love, grounded in the Christian faith, can easily overcome man-made institutional differences.

THE WEDDING I FORGOT

It was a beach wedding, complete with the most unusual decorations I have ever seen, but it proved to be one of the most memorable weddings I have ever conducted.

Friends of mine own a summer cottage in Invermere, British Columbia, a three-hour drive from Calgary, Alberta, through the mountains. For many years, they have summered there at the lakeside where their condominium is located. They have made many friends at the cottage community through the years including an older couple who lived together for more than a dozen years without the benefit of clergy. It seems that the mother of the woman in question was well into her 90s and had been pressuring her daughter to "sign the paper that would make her an honest woman." My friends offered the name a of a minister (myself) who would likely do the honours so the couple decided to surprise the woman's mother with a special lakeside ceremony. I made the necessary legal arrangements to officiate at a provincially approved wedding in British Columbia.

Rev. John W. Friesen, Ph.D., D.Min., D.R.S.

The wedding was scheduled to take place during the midst of the warm summer season, a rare event in the Calgary, Alberta area, and perhaps the sunny days affected my memory. In any event, I arrived at my friends' cottage a week early. Trying to be sensitive about the matter, at the appropriate time, my hosts asked me, "Are you here for the wedding? Well, perhaps you remember that it is next week and you are just a bit early." Embarrassed, I visited with my friends, then left for home.

The next week went by uneventfully, and on Saturday, the day of the wedding, I was eating a leisurely lunch when my friends from Invermere telephoned, "How come you are still at home? When are you coming to the wedding? It is supposed to start in an hour?"

I was in shock; this was *not* the professional behaviour on which I prided myself! My friends immediately assured me that my late arrival would not greatly affect the event since it was supposed to be very informal anyway. Still, they suggested just a bit sarcastically, that perhaps I ought to get started.

Now I was *really* embarrassed! I quickly changed my clothes and made the trip to Invermere on my motorcycle as fast as possible. I was even impeded a bit by being followed by an unsuspecting law enforcement officer in a police car for a half hour to make sure I would not speed. When I arrived at the beach location, appropriately fitted with my clerical collar, I announced, "Is there anyone here who wants to get married?"

The bridal couple immediately spoke up and the bride's elderly mother was ecstatic! "It's about time," she proclaimed. I would venture to say that she was the most enthusiastic person present. Quickly the carefully lined surfboards leaning against some trees were turned around. They had been appropriately decorated with flowers and inscribed with the names of the bride and groom. This made a memorable backdrop to a beautiful lakeside wedding.

Since then I have never missed a scheduled wedding.

VI.
SAYING GOODBYE

MY FIRST FUNERAL

Believe it or not, a funeral can be a beautiful and memorable experience. It need not always be sad, that is, if the minister knows what he is doing.

There was a faithful elderly couple in my first country church—Steinreich Mennonite Brethren Church, and in due time the husband grew ill and was hospitalized. I visited him there and met his extended family, most of whom lived in the area and attended surrounding churches. The parents preferred our small country church because it comprised the congregation with which they had been raised.

One evening the elderly man's condition grew more severe, and his physician indicated to the family that he would probably not make it through the night. There was little the doctor could do but advise family members to prepare for a funeral. They therefore met with me to make preliminary plans for the funeral service.

Up till then, the arrangement had been that every morning the couple's daughter stopped at the family home picked up her mother for the ride to the hospital to visit her father. The mother took it upon herself to wait for her daughter on her house porch in her old rocking chair. Appearing to be in good health, although also aged, this woman preferred to spend each day at the hospital with her dying husband. On the evening of her father's passing, I got a late telephone call from the daughter informing me that her father was in a very weakened condition. His doctor did not expect him to live through the night. She wanted my advice: should she tell her mother or wait until the next morning? Although completely inexperienced in such matters, I used my best judgment and told her it might be best to wait until morning. That way her mother might be able to get some sleep. Why provide her with such unfortunate news so late in the evening?

The next morning when the daughter arrived at her mother's house, she found her mother waiting on the porch in her rocking chair, apparently ready to go to the hospital. To the daughter's shock and surprise, she discovered that her mother had passed away. She parted this world while waiting for her daughter. Later that morning, unaware that his wife had passed on, the elderly gentleman went to be with the Lord. Now we had to plan a *double* funeral. A question that buzzed around in my head during this turn of events was, "Did the couple really know about each other's passing even though no one had told them?" Perhaps they did.

The thought of conducting my first funeral as a double funeral was a bit challenging, so I approached the family about seeking the assistance of a retired minister who was known to the family. I was relieved when they consented because I could really use some advice. We soon discovered that would be necessary to hold the service in a larger church in the area because the couple was well known in the surrounding community. Although I had graduated from two Bible colleges, neither one offered a course on the practicalities of ministry—like conducting weddings, baptism, Holy Communion, or funerals. Instead, we almost exclusively studied the Bible. In addition, this was a Mennonite Church, and the conference was not attuned to providing beginning ministers with any kind of manual or specific guidance. I think it was assumed that they would stumble through on their own. Right about then I was wishing I had paid more attention to the proceedings at funerals I had attended as a youth!

The funeral service went well, except for one thing. Operating out of a facility unfamiliar to me, my retired assistant and I assumed that we would lead the funeral entourage out of the church by the rear door. It seemed logical to do so. However, as we neared the middle of the building we glanced back, only to see the undertaker guide the caskets out of the side door. Needless to say, we were very embarrassed, and could not comprehend why the director of the funeral home had chosen to make his own exit. When queried, he informed us that he was very familiar with the church and it was always their practice to use the side entrance as an exit for funeral processions. Apparently, the two of us should somehow have known about this custom.

Despite this gaff, what I will always remember most about this funeral was the beautiful transition by which a faithful Christian couple was joined together in death.

ASSISTANT FUNERAL DIRECTOR

Being a minister to a country church congregation can often both be complex and interesting because of the obvious lack of resources and conveniences. A funeral director once phoned me to inform me of the death of a parishioner. He asked me to meet him at the home of the deceased as soon as I could. Upon arriving, I quickly realized why he had called me; he was unable to lift the body of the deceased into the hearse by himself and he needed my help.

"Well, don't just stand there," he said when I arrived. "Grab hold; you don't think I can do this all by myself, do you?"

I "grabbed hold," as he suggested, marveling at the difficulty of handling the body of the deceased. I was not prepared to handle such a limp and delicate payload. I also wondered again, why I wasn't prepared for this kind of responsibility during Bible College training.

This particular funeral has a sad corollary. The deceased woman had been estranged from her daughter for many years, but the daughter *did* attend the funeral. When the casket was opened for viewing after the service the daughter was so overcome with remorse, that she threw herself on her mother's body, and sobbed convulsively. After a few minutes, the pallbearers tore the daughter away, still overcome by her grief.

I resolved right at that moment that when it came time for my parents to approach heaven, I would be at peace with them.

It was a promise I kept.

AN IMPRESSIVE FUNERAL

I have heard of many reasons why people take up fellowship in the Christian community, but this story offers an unusual twist. I once met a man who was very active in a local Calgary congregation. I was curious, as I always am, how an individual with virtually no previous church background, manifested such commitment. This was that man's story.

One day the individual in question attended a funeral of a woman who had lived in his neighbourhood. He and his wife did not really know the woman, and as it turned out, neither did anyone else. In the first place, there were scarcely 20 people present at the funeral and most of them appeared to have attended out of courtesy to the women's memory. The minister had obviously never met the woman and had nothing personal to say about her in his eulogy. The minister invited anyone present to mount the pulpit to express their thoughts about the deceased, but none of those present availed themselves of the opportunity. Apparently, no one knew anything about the deceased except that she had lived in the neighbourhood.

When my acquaintance went home, he decided that when it came time for him to die, at least a few individuals would have memories of his life. He would see to that! He promptly looked up the name of the nearest church, and began attending services. He enrolled in membership classes, testified to an acceptable form of conversion experience, and made it a point to become acquainted with members of the church. He and his wife engaged in a wide variety of church activities, and eventually he was even elected to the church board. Now his legacy was assured; *someone* would have *something* to say about him at his funeral!

I believe that there are more valid reasons for joining a Christian fellowship, but who is to say.

LOYALTY AMID TRAGEDY

In every congregation there are individuals or even entire families who serve as positive Christian models, whether or not they know it. I believe we should be grateful for their ministry and occasionally let them know that we appreciate them.

I met one such an individual at Camp Creek EUB Church where I was minister. Her story was a history of turmoil and tragedy, yet her testimony remained steadfast. Her husband, on the other hand, refused to have anything to do with the church. However, he did offer me, the student minister, part-time farm work operating various kinds of farm machinery when I was in financial need, which was an opportunity that I greatly appreciated. It helped to supplement my meager income as a student minister, although I am quite sure that it was nearly impossible to obtain reliable farm help.

Prior to my arrival at the congregation I learned that Grace and her husband had lost their married daughter to cancer and because of a family disagreement, the widowed husband refused to allow the grandparents to visit his three motherless children. I also learned that Grace's oldest son, Leon, was stricken with polio while a freshman in college. Therefore, he was confined to his bed, 24/7, with the bed set up so it operated in motion eight hours a day in to provide a measure of exercise for Leon. His mother took care of him, graciously performing a duty that would occupy nearly all of her time and keep her constantly on watch.

My pastoral predecessor made arrangements to play chess with Leon once a month, and it was expected that I would carry on this practice, which I did with much interest. My visit with Leon gave Grace a much-needed opportunity to socialize with her peers as a member of the local women's church mission circle. During Grace's timeout, Leon not only sharpened my skills at playing chess, but he also influenced my interest in watching professional baseball on television. His favourite team was the *Kansas City A's*, which was later moved to Los Angeles.

Despite all of these tragedies in her life, Grace never wavered in her faith, and indeed encouraged me whenever I came to visit. I was amazed that anyone could bear up as well as she did.

Leon's younger brother, Richard, was married during my ministry at this church, and a year later the couple had a child who died soon after birth. Although I had moved on to another parish by this time, I often thought of Grace and wondered how she would hold up in the face of yet another tragic loss.

The news was always positive; Grace truly loved the Lord and trusted in His leading. Years later I learned that Leon had passed away; polio had taken his life. Ironically, his mother Grace, his faithful nurse, passed away a month later.

"…Blessed are the dead who die in the Lord…for their deeds will follow them (Revelation 14:13 NIV)."

A RURAL CHRISTIAN STALWART

His funeral drew more than five hundred people, yet he never graduated high school, and rarely left Atchison County, Kansas where he grew up. He was a farmer who worked hard, married and raised a family, dealt honestly with his neighbours, and loyally supported his church.

Henry Bodenhausen of Cummings, Kansas, inherited his first piece of land from his father, who inherited the land from *his* father, who was part of a group of European settlers who migrated to the Cummings, Kansas area a few generations back. The family brought their German ancestry to America that included a strong work ethic, blatant honesty in business dealings, and an implicit faith in God that things would always work out.

Education was deemed important in the Bodenhausen family, and being the oldest, Henry was expected to attend high school. It was six miles (nine kilometres) to Effingham High School. The first day of grade nine, Henry dutifully got on the bus, and headed to school. By noon that day, Henry decided he had obtained enough education; after all, there was work to be done at home and school was taking up valuable time. Henry was not exactly sure which route the bus had taken in the ride to Effingham, but he knew that if he headed down the railway track that ran from Effingham to near his home, he would be able to locate the family farm. Slowly, on foot, he followed the track for six miles (10 kilometres) to his home, never again, to return to high school. He later confessed that it did not seem to make much difference to his farming success, whether or not he completed high school, and I believed him.

Henry's faith took him through the various struggles that often troubled farmers on the Great Plains—late spring planting, heavy rains and snows that washed out sections of farmland, hail, and drought. One particularly dry summer, when the church well went dry, the church trustees were hard at work "water witching" for a water supply. This unique process consists of someone with "the gift," tightly holding a willow branch in his hand over the area where it is hoped water will be found. If water *is* present, the willow branch will apparently bob up and down, and then it will be the place to drill for water. Sometimes the process works, but in this instance, using that method, the drillers drilled several dry holes and found no water. The drought was real.

As the drought dragged into the late summer months, many farmers grew worried about the lack of moisture, and were sure that their dried out crops would never mature. During some of the heavy conversations about the sad state of affairs, Uncle Henry assured everyone that things would turn out okay It was simply a matter of faith. "After all," he said, "my grandfather could remember when it rained!"

Henry Bodenhausen lived well into his sixties, and when he died the community felt a keen sense of loss. His funeral could not be held in his home church because it was too small; it only seated 150 people and his funeral drew more than three times that number. In fact, the funeral home in Atchison, Kansas, where the service was held, was packed to the limit. Everyone, it seemed, wanted to pay tribute to this simple, hard-working farmer who was a model to both city and rural folks around. A year after his death I was asked to pen a poem in his memory.

ODE TO UNCLE HENRY

by John W. Friesen, written in honour of Henry Bodenhausen (1900-1965)

Through customs we express our lives,
Our deepest woes, our joys, our sighs,
And one such thought great truth belies,
In loving memory.

I'd like to offer such a thought,
In memory of a man who sought,
To practice just what Jesus taught,
And in His memory.

A year ago, God bid him rest,
Life challenged him, he stood the test,
And heav'n was his, God's very best,
A comforting memory.

As "Uncle Henry" he was known,
And by his deeds he set a tone,
That spoke of life by faith alone,
A durable memory.

One summer we had quite a drought,
That it could rain, there was some doubt,
But Henry said the corn would sprout,
An impressive memory.

His faithful testimony stayed,
For from his goal, he never strayed,
He worked, and spoke, and sang and prayed,

A consistent memory.

And sometimes when my tasks seemed long,
I'd visit with my brother strong,
And come away, my heart in song,
A happy memory.

O Christian, it's not what you say,
Or who you are, or what your pay,
But *what* you are from day to day,
That builds a memory.

These lines were penned that we might take,
This challenge for our Savior's sake,
That as we walk, build in our wake,
A lasting memory.

We dedicate these lines to one,
Who ran the race, the crown has won,
Who drew his strength from God's own Son,
In loving memory.

VII.
DIVERSITY IN MINISTRY

AH, THOSE COUNTRY CHRISTIANS!

Ministers in rural communities often play a variety of roles, and my experience has been no different. I discovered this in a real way when I was serving the Corning and New Eden Evangelical United Brethren congregations in north central Kansas.

One spring I was asked to deliver the graduation address at the local elementary school, and I was honoured to do so. I armed myself with an appropriate number of jokes and wise sayings and took my place on the platform with the four local school trustees, all of them men. Among other lines I used, I told the attending assembly that as one gets older, the roots of one's hair grow deeper. If they reach grey matter, the hair turns grey. If the searching roots find no grey matter, the hair all falls out. Having stated this "fact," the audience broke into great peels of laughter. I did not feel that the joke was *that* funny until I looked around and noticed that every member of the platform party was bald!

While visiting an elderly Kansas couple in their home for lunch after church, we chanced to talk about musical instruments—guitars, in particular.

"Just how old is your guitar, Reverend?" the old-timer wanted to know. "It was a mail order guitar in 1949," I replied. "Well, he said, "I have one upstairs that was ordered in 1948! How do you like that?"

Then he winked, grinned broadly, and advised me; "Reverend, never start in a lying contest!"

In Bible College homiletics class we were taught to write out our sermons carefully, but never take full notes to the pulpit, only an outline. Our instructor, the late Rev. Jacob Epp, told us that we should be so familiar with our material that we would never actually just read a sermon to the congregation. We should only have before us a list of keywords and then expand on them. I can remember only two times in my career when I mounted the pulpit *without any notes*, both of them quite unnerving moments. I survived both of them, only to be more careful in the future.

One Sunday I forgot my Bible when I left the Corning Church, only to retrieve it from a concerned Kansas farmer the following week. It turns out that he found my sermon notes in the Bible and carefully went over them.

"I am amazed," he informed me, "that you got all them ideas from so few words." I felt it was my duty to apprise him of the instructions I had received in Bible college homiletics class, and he seemed appreciative.

At Corning, I presided at one of my most sorrowful funerals—a triple funeral resulting from a horrible car accident. It seems that a young man in a speeding car drove through a stop sign and took the lives of three people, but not his own. What a memory to have to live with! The deceased were a young mother and two children—her son and her nephew. The tiny church did not hold nearly all of the people who attended, and the platform was so full of flowers there was really no place for me to stand. As I recall, I gained standing room only between two tall bouquets of flowers and never sat down between program items. There simply was no room!

Tragedies like this seem to stamp an indelible mark on my soul. I know that the themes of the Old Testament book, Job, is about why Christians suffer, but even those wise words sometimes seem inadequate when it comes to comforting hurting believers.

Only God can heal a broken heart.

MULTICULTURALISM IN ITS INFANCY

I was far ahead of the Canadian government when the country instituted its policy on multiculturalism in 1971! It's a nice feeling to think that you are ahead of the times, and this incident was as close as I came.

In 1963 when I was a part-time instructor at Highland University in northeast Kansas, two students who were "in love" approached me and since I was their sociology instructor, they wanted to know what I thought their chances of happiness were if they married. They were particularly worried about the reaction of their families when they found out. The young man in question was the "all American boy," and the young woman was from Iran.

My response to them was the same as it would be today. I told them, "If you think your love is strong enough to withstand the onslaught of criticism and disapproval that you will no doubt encounter along the way, go for it. However, do not underestimate the force of prejudice, racism, and discrimination that you will encounter—even from your loved ones. Be sure you know that this is what you want! Your decision will affect the rest of your life."

Marriage is like that; if a couple with cultural differences have a strong enough love, grounded, of course, by their faith in God, they should be able to withstand pretty well any force of opposition.

ETHNIC INVASION

Being born into an ethnic Mennonite background awarded me with the ability to speak three languages—Low German at home, High German in church, and English with outsiders. My use of High German has deteriorated severely through the years since I have had very little opportunity to use it. My familiarity with Low German, however, prevails to this day since I used the language a great deal in speaking with my parents. Now that they are gone, I find that my ease in speaking that language is also waning. Linguistic experts like to point out that you have to use a language in your daily home life to maintain it, and I quite agree with them.

Being bilingual can also offer a few complications. When I was studying at Tabor College, my advisor, Professor Walter Kleinsasser, suggested that I try hard to drop the "Germanisms" from my essays.

"You still appear to be thinking in German," he would say. "You have a tendency to dangle verbs at the end of your sentences!" Having been raised with a Hutterite background, Professor Kleinsasser was well aware of what it means to think in German. I took his advice to heart and began to watch my use of language a bit more. My wife, Virginia, informs me that whenever I get excited, my Mennonite accent still comes out quite pronouncedly.

Shortly after I was born, my parents left the Saskatchewan Mennonite community of their birth for employment opportunities in British Columbia. Growing up in a non-Mennonite community in Trail, B.C., my siblings and I grew up speaking Low German at home and English in school and with neighbourhood children. There was no High German language church to attend in the area. The arrangement worked very well except as a very young boy I thought that Low German was my family's own private language. In fact, I thought that every family probably had their own private language!

After a few successful years in British Columbia, my parents were able to afford annual visits to their home community in Saskatchewan. I was about six years old when this first occurred, and on attending my initial reunion with members of the extended family, I discovered to my dismay that everyone present was speaking Low German! Quietly I drew my father aside and shared my shock and surprise with him.

"Dad," I said, "Why are they all speaking *our* language?" My father smiled and assured me that it was okay. After all, we were all part of the same family! Later I found out that members of the Mennonite community, who were *not* part of our extended family, *also* spoke our language. I felt quite invaded. Now there could be no family secrets.

Meaningful Moments in Ministry

Despite my father's assurance that the nuclear family is not an entity to itself, it took me quite a while to learn that the human community is even larger than the Mennonite whole. I would say that this is a concept on which I am still working.

ENCOUNTER WITH PREJUDICE

The North American Midwest is often painted with the brush of small-box thinking, particularly when it comes to such matters as racism, prejudice, discrimination, and intolerance. Having grown up in this region, I am quite familiar with a number of variations pertaining to this phenomenon. My story, however, is unique.

While studying in Kansas, I was once pastor to two tiny EUB rural congregations located just four miles (six kilometres) apart. Both congregations owned a minister's residence (rectory, manse, or parsonage), a symbol of their past size and financial capabilities. Now, however, the minister was expected to reside in *one* of the homes while the other was rented out to provide additional revenue to assist an already over stretched budget. When the rental property became available for new tenants an advertisement was placed in a local paper. The phone numbers in the ad were those of the chairman of the church board of trustees and the minister.

One day our telephone rang and the individual on the other end of the line requested to see the advertised rental property. I indicated to him that it was a church parsonage and if he rented the property, he might be living next to a church. That information did not turn him off, and he requested to inspect the property. Then he informed *me* that I should know that he was Black (African American). I assured him that this made no difference to me and I would arrange for him to inspect the property with the church board of trustees the following day. After I hung up the telephone, I called the trustees to make the appointment. I informed them that the man in question said to be sure to tell them that he was Black. I did so, and I was not prepared for the reaction I received.

This event took place during the sixties, at the height of the civil rights movement in the United States. In keeping with the times, the trustees firmly informed me that they were not ready to rent the house to "no Black!" I informed *them* that if the inquirer met rental conditions and he was refused, I would resign as pastor of the church! Later that day I wondered if I had been a bit too hasty. After all, I did have three children to support. Still, I was prepared to stand by my convictions.

The following day the church trustees and I met with our would-be renter who introduced himself as William Smith (not his real name), and mentioned that he had grown up in the area. In fact, he stated, his father, Jimmie Smith, was well known in the district. He used to work for some of the local farmers.

The atmosphere in the room immediately became less tense as one of the trustees spoke out. "You're Jimmie Smith's son? Well, that's good to know. I knew your father and he was a hard worker. Lots of people around here would tell you that!"

He turned to me and said, "Reverend, if this man wants to rent the parsonage, he can have it. He's Jimmie Smith's boy!"

I was a bit shocked at this sudden change in attitude. Suddenly it didn't matter that William was Black. He became human because his critics had new information. I couldn't help wondering that if this kind of experience could happen to all North Americans, maybe there wouldn't be such things as racism, prejudice, and discrimination.

INSIGHTS FROM THE DOUKHOBORS

Combining the careers of clergyman and academic has always been a rich source of information and even inspiration for me. I found I could use illustrations from academic research in my sermons, and stories from my church experience as classroom material.

Growing up as a boy in southern British Columbia, I became acquainted with Doukhobor communities by travelling with my parents to Doukhobor communal villages to buy fruit and vegetables. Doukhobors originated in Russia, where, among other skills, they learned to nurture first class gardens. Unfortunately, many fellow Canadians do not understand their religious beliefs.

In Russia, the Doukhobors were as an undesirable sect because their leaders objected to recent changes to the beliefs, practices, and policies of the 17th century Russian Orthodox Church. Because of their opposition to the new practices of the state church, the Doukhobors were nicknamed, "Spirit Wrestlers," implying that they were fighting against the Spirit of God. Doukhobors endorsed the name, insisting that they wrestled "in the Spirit of God," to grow closer to the ideal that God wanted for them. In 1899, due to ongoing religious persecution, 7,500 of them immigrated to Canada at the invitation of Clifford Sifton, then Minister of the Interior.

To their sad surprise, the Doukhobors experienced a rather hostile welcome in Canada over the next century. At first, the 57 communal villages the Doukhobors established in eastern Saskatchewan were viewed with curiosity, but when the Doukhobors objected to swearing allegiance to the Crown in order to register their homesteads with government agents, public opposition grew. The Doukhobors also objected to sending their children to public schools where they would learn about justified violence and war and perhaps be corrupted by bad morals. Within just a few years of their arrival in Canada, Doukhobor lands were confiscated by the federal government and assigned to other settlers.

By 1912, most Doukhobors had settled in British Columbia where they purchased land that had already been registered with the federal government. Now it would no longer be necessary for them to swear allegiance to what they perceived to be a man-made institution, not necessarily blessed by God.

Rev. John W. Friesen, Ph.D., D.Min., D.R.S.

Doukhobor theology is made up of several fundamental beliefs. First, they reject the existence of the organized church and the notion of ordained clergy. They insist that God speaks personally to each seeker and except for maintaining informal fellowships, or prayer groups, there is no need for the written word like the Bible, except as a resource. They believe that God communicates His will directly, and on a daily basis to those who seek His presence. The Bible then becomes a resource, but it is not viewed as outlining a pattern for daily living. Doukhobors believe in equality of the sexes—that is, anyone, male or female, can lead a fellowship meeting. They are also pacifists, to the point of not killing animals for food, and they reject icons. In Russia, and originally in Canada, they lived communally until their way of life was destroyed by Canadian government action in 1939.

In 1984, I began a five-year research project to write a book about Doukhobors, with my Doukhobor friend, Michael M. Verigin, secretary of the United Doukhobors of Alberta. The book was published in 1989 and republished in 1996 by Borealis Press of Ottawa, Ontario, and is entitled, *The Community Doukhobors: A People in Transition.*

A vital component in researching the Doukhobor belief system was to conduct interviews with knowledgeable members of the faith. I will never forget my first interview with the late 80-year-old George Maloff of Cowley, Alberta. When I asked him how he would summarize the belief system of the Doukhobors he wisely replied, "John, don't ask me such questions. Watch how I live, and you will soon discover what I believe. Don't talk about your beliefs, *live them!*"

These words have lingered in my mind for many years. I have concluded that those of us raised in Evangelical communities probably *do* talk too much; we claim too much, and our lives cannot always catch up to our claims.

A decade and a half ago, I was accumulating information for a book on world religions. The resultant book is entitled, *Pick One: A User-Friendly Guide to Religion.* (Calgary, AB: Temeron/Detselig, 1995). I enjoyed doing the research, and when I was ready to take the

106 *Meaningful Moments in Ministry*

manuscript to the publisher, my wife Virginia, asked me which one of the belief systems I had studied, most appealed to me. I replied that if I had to do things over again, I would probably become a Doukhobor or a Quaker because of their insistence that individuals talk less about their faith, and instead try to live it—a strong reminder of a familiar biblical phrase, "Thus, by their fruit you will recognize them" (Matthew 7:20 NIV).

IT'S OUR TRADITION

As the world continues to diminish in size, thanks to increased means of communication, it is sometimes easy to forget the origins of specific customs or beliefs. This is particularly the case when a lot of time passes and the human mind is influenced by a multiplicity of intervening factors.

We encountered one such incident on one of our 16 visits to the American southwest. Ardent students of pueblo Indian history, over the years we tried to visit all 19 pueblos located in New Mexico. As we toured these villages, we captured our experiences on film, but always with the permission of pueblo authorities.

While visiting Acoma Pueblo in New Mexico, we were accompanied by guide who gave us permission to take photographs of the various buildings. When we approached the local Catholic Church, however, she told us not to take a photograph of it. When I inquired as to the reason for her refusal she simply replied, "It's our tradition."

I tried gently to remind our guide that her historical Aboriginal religion predated missionary efforts of the Roman Catholic Church, so how could this particular Christian church be part of *her* tradition? I also pointed out that the Christian faith was probably more akin to *our* tradition than hers, so why couldn't I take a picture of the church?

What was her response to this academic line of reasoning?

"Whatever; just don't take any pictures of the church!"

I didn't take any pictures of the church, and concluded that cultural beliefs do not necessarily have to portray rational consistency!

REVERENCE FOR SACRED WRITINGS

During the years when I was teaching courses on multiculturalism at the University of Calgary, I sponsored field trips to related sites such as local museums with ethnic exhibits, the Stoney (Nakoda Sioux) Indian Reserve, an Italian Roman Catholic Church, a Hutterite Colony, and the Sikh temple. Over the years, my students and I visited the Sikh temple at least a dozen times and became good friends with the local priest, the Reverend Pashura Singh. A very accommodating man, Reverend Singh would walk us through Sikh history and beliefs, demonstrate aspects of Sikh culture, and even serve us a light lunch.

Our host informed us that the Sikh faith, guided by the vision of Guru Nanak (1469—1504), originated in the Punjab in India about the time of the Protestant Reformation. Guru Nanak was the first of ten Sikh gurus, and the principles he advocated were simple: (i) practice love, not hollow rituals; (ii) deeds alone are valued, not empty words; (iii) live honestly; (iv) physical renunciation is of no value; and, (v) service is the only form of true worship.

It was the fifth Guru, Guru Arjan (1563—1606), who saw the need to assemble writings that would contain basic Sikh teachings for future generations. These became the Holy Scriptures of the Sikh faith. Borrowing from the writings of holy men with Islam or Hindu connections, and committed to the principle that all individuals are equal, Guru Arjan was careful to include the thoughts of individuals who represented all castes. He also accepted all prevailing names for God as equally valid, and promoted the principle that all languages are valid in offering praise to God.

When a Sikh enters the temple, the protocol calls for the wearing of a head covering and removal of one's shoes. The scriptures are located at the front of the temple under a canopy. Each morning, before sunrise, the priest is required to bring the scriptures out of a special room and place them under the canopy. At sundown, he returns the scriptures to the special room. When delivering the scriptures to the canopy, the priest randomly opens the holy book, and points to a verse anywhere on the page he has opened. The verse he points to can become his guiding thought for the day. The content of the Sikh scriptures is written much in the order of the Book of Psalms, so the selected verse is usually of the genre that offers praise or thanksgiving to God.

Adherents to the Sikh faith are permitted to have copies of the scriptures (or parts thereof) in their homes, but if they choose to do so, the scriptures must be placed in a separate room (or closet) at night and brought out at sunrise. When removed from the closet, the scriptures may be consulted for inspiration.

I have often wondered what would happen if Christians had such high regard for the Holy Bible!

UNDESERVED FORGIVENESS

Canada prides herself on being a multicultural nation, apparently always ready to accommodate newcomers and encourage them to maintain their cultural identities. On October 8, 1971, then Prime Minister Pierre Elliott Trudeau rose in the House of Common to announce support for a new policy on multiculturalism. This policy read in part, "The Government of Canada will support all of Canada's cultures and will seek to assist, resources permitting, the development of those cultural groups which have demonstrated a desire and effort to continue to develop, a capacity to grow and contribute to Canada, as well as a clear need for assistance."

Canada's history reveals that ethnic minorities have not always been treated very well, and the Chinese community is a good example.

Between 1876 and 1884, 17,027 Chinese were admitted to Canada at the port of Victoria, British Columbia. Here they joined about three thousand Chinese who had already entered the country from California after the famed California Gold Rush. The new immigrants soon discovered that they were not allowed to work on public projects because of anti-Chinese sentiment and they were unable to find other work. Ironically, the federal government was in desperate need of cheap labour in building the transcontinental railroad, so they hired Chinese workers. The work was exceedingly dangerous, and one out of every four Chinese workers died by accident completing the railway through the Canadian Rocky Mountains. When the project was complete, however, the Chinese were no longer wanted.

In 1885, the Canadian government passed its first anti-Chinese legislation, consisting of a head tax of fifty dollars on each Chinese immigrant entering the country. This amount increased to $100 in 1901, and to $500 in 1905. Chinese citizens were discouraged from enrolling their children in public schools, and their right to vote in any kind of election was cancelled. In the meantime, they were subjected to many forms of racism, prejudice, and discrimination.

As the years went by, things changed slowly for Canadian Chinese citizens as prejudice against them gradually diminished. It seems that the federal multicultural policy may yet serve its purpose.

Sometime ago the National Film Board of Canada released a film entitled, "Golden Mountain," in which the story of the Chinese in Canada was documented. In one scene, an interviewer speaks with an elderly Chinese individual about the treatment of his people in this country. The interviewee dismisses the question with a statement something like this; "That is all in the past. We do not worry about that. We simply want to take our proper place in Canadian society and seek to make a contribution."

After reviewing the treatment of Chinese in Canada over the past century, that indeed is an admirable attitude. Jesus once said something about this kind of situation when approached on the subject by the disciple Peter. "Peter said, 'Lord, how many times shall I forgive my brother or sister who sins against me? Up to seven times?' Jesus answered, 'I tell you, not seven times, but seventy-seven times'" (Matthew 18: 21b-22 NIV).

The Chinese in Canada seem to function in accordance with this concept.

TRUE FAMILY WORSHIP

Whenever my wife Virginia and I travel in North America, we make it a point to find a church for Sunday worship—usually a United Methodist Church. Several years ago, while in Ambridge, Pennsylvania, on a Sunday morning, we noted that it was nearly eleven o'clock, and we would have to find a United Methodist Church. We checked with a local bystander who informed us that such a church was "just around the corner." After identifying the building by the sign outside, we noted that it comprised a large house that had been made-over into a church. Somewhat uncertain about what to expect, we made our way into the church; then discovered that we were going to be worshipping with an African American congregation.

Never having worshipped with Black folks before, we were in for some pleasant surprises. To begin with, the minister was both organist and song leader, and the congregational singing was hearty and joyous. When the congregants cited the Apostles' Creed, it was said responsively and with great enthusiasm. The minister would offer a line, and the congregation would repeat it. It went something like this. The minister would say, "I believe in God, the Father Almighty," and the congregation would echo the words in chorus.

When we arrived back home to the Morley United Church, we tried to motivate our Stoney (Nakoda Sioux) friends to adopt the enthusiastic custom, but it turned out to be difficult! After six months of persistence, we did finally manage to bring the level of congregational

Rev. John W. Friesen, Ph.D., D.Min., D.R.S. 111

response to just past a whisper. They were just too shy.

Meanwhile, back to Ambridge and the morning (pastoral) prayer. Instead of the minister offering a prayer on behalf of the congregation, there were four prayers—each offered by an individual of a different generation—a child prayed, then a teen, followed by a young adult, and then an elder. When a teenager got up to sing a solo, her father stood at the back of the church loudly encouraging her by shouting as she sang, "You go, girl; sing it!"

The sermon that day in Ambridge was somewhat scolding in tone; it sounded like the minister was unhappy with some element of congregational response and was reprimanding them for their lack of participation. We were later informed that such an approach is common among African American churches, and the people take reproach as an expected charge from the clergy. In this case, any negative aura cast by the minister's harsh preaching style was easily overshadowed by the enthusiasm of the worshippers. I got to thinking; a good theological reprimand may be just what is needed occasionally in today's churches.

After a brief conversation with the minister of the congregation, we looked forward to planning a return visit. Our spirits had been uplifted and we could hardly wait to share our experience with the folks back home. We felt a bit like the Israelites when they returned home and had their first worship service after having been exiled in Babylon for 70 years.

Nehemiah 8:12 (NIV) puts it this way: "Then all the people went away to eat and drink, to send portions of food and to celebrate with great joy, because they now understood the words that had been made known to them."

GRANDPA, GRANDPA; LOOK AT ALL THE INDIANS!

After growing up with and working with Aboriginal people for so many years, I have become quite accustomed to witnessing the tremendous ignorance that exists about their ways in the minds of the public. In fact, thanks to the hard sell of Christian European ways by missionaries of long ago, many young people of Indian descent are also quite unfamiliar with the ways of their ancestors. To remedy this, many colleges and universities have established Native studies departments that offer courses dealing with historical, spiritual, and educational aspects of traditional AmerIndian ways. My wife, Virginia and I have often taught courses on aspects of plains Indian history, education, and art at Old Sun College on the Blackfoot (Blackfeet) Indian Reserve at Gleichen, Alberta, on behalf of the Department of Communication and Culture at the University of Calgary.

During our 25 year on-again, off-again term of ministry at the Morley United Church on the Stoney (Nakoda Sioux) Indian Reserve, located west of Calgary, we learned a great deal about the local culture which we tried to incorporate into the various courses we offered. While at Morley, Virginia photographed and assembled a slide show of the activities of the church and one year arranged to show them to the congregation at the Christmas Eve Service. This particular evening, our daughter, Karen, and her three children attended. Rachel, Karen's three-year-old daughter, was seated next to the late John Snow, Chief of the local Wesley Band.

As the show got underway, Rachel's eyes opened wide with glee as she observed the various aspects of congregational life at the Morley Church over the past year. Finally, when viewing a slide of our church choir, she could hold her enthusiasm no longer and loudly exclaimed to me, "Grandpa, Grandpa, look at all the Indians!"

It was more than Chief John Snow could bear.

"Where does she think she is?" he roared with laughter, and poor little Rachel suddenly knew that she must have said something inappropriate.

The punch line of the story is that people can sometimes be quite unaware that they are involved in culturally different circumstances.

Rev. John W. Friesen, Ph.D., D.Min., D.R.S.

I am happy to report that Rachel, now married and graduated from the Kings' College in Edmonton, Alberta, has made up for her lack of familiarity with Native ways.

EVERYBODY SING

During our years at Morley United Church on the Stoney (Nakoda Sioux) Indian Reserve my wife, Virginia, has often organized an impromptu choir for special occasions. The choir performs at Easter, Christmas, and Thanksgiving. Usually about a dozen or so individuals show up for practice, and after two or three practices we think they sound pretty good.

As time went on, the choir members decided that it would improve the presence of the choir if they wore robes during performances. "It would be really nice," several of the women ventured. "Will you try to get us some choir robes?"

We were most fortunate in our quest because at this time in local church history, choir robes were out of style. People in congregations in the nearby city of Calgary were featuring a come-as-you-are focus, so that choir members were no differently dressed than their peers in the pew. After a few telephone calls to other United Church of Canada congregations, we found we had more choir robes than we needed— at least so we thought. We originally looked for about a dozen choir robes and ended up with more than forty.

When word spread that there were choir robes to wear for performances, the number of choir members rose quickly. Everyone, it seemed, wanted to wear a choir robe. Thus, when it was announced that the choir would sing during the service, more than thirty people took their place on the platform and put on robes. Even a few teenagers and younger children joined the choir, even though they had not attended practice sessions to learn the new choir songs!

Wearing a choir robe was viewed by members of the Stoney church choir as a very special honour. I am sure that God was pleased with the resulting music!

I WANT TO GIVE YOU SOMETHING

Not long ago, my wife, Virginia and I were invited to provide leadership for a weekend camp designed for a group called 55+. Since the farm I grew up on was much like a summer camp, I was not particularly fond of summer camps, however, we accepted the invitation because some very special friends invited us. Over the years both of us have developed a special liking for central heating, running water, and warm showers, not all of them facilities which some camps feature. To our joy, we discovered that this one did!

The weekend camp sponsored by the Church of God (Anderson, Indiana) is an affiliation I have known since my teen years. Several of my siblings and myself were baptized in that denomination and I have always had a distinct fondness for their taking me in.

While preparing for the weekend, Virginia and I planned a series of seminars that we thought would be relevant for a 55+ age group. We decided to talk about forgiveness and the grace of God, family life, and meaningful retirement. We had a great time discussing these topics with "older folk," many of whose experiences we could readily identify with. During discussions at meal times and during coffee breaks we discovered that many members of the group were facing near heartbreak experiences such as the empty nest, being estranged from family members, or having to move to smaller, unfamiliar surroundings. For three days, we listened, consoled, prayed with, and counselled our new acquaintances and fell into bed each night happy, but thoroughly exhausted.

The arrangement was that we served the weekend camp without remuneration, and no doubt, some of the campers discovered this. As camp broke up and everyone was leaving, one gentleman came up to me and said, "I want to give you something."

Reaching into the trunk of his car, he pulled out a 25-foot (7.6 metres) coil of rope, one half inch (1.27 centimetres) in diameter, and handed it to me. "My brother makes these," he said, "I would like you to have one. You never know when a coil of rope might come in handy!"

He was right. I'll probably never know when that piece of rope will come in handy. It is situated undisturbed in a desk drawer in my office, but whenever I open that drawer, the kind thought behind it wells up in my mind. My new friend wanted to "give me something." In the same sense, I would like these memories to be my gift to someone.

It is never the nature of the gift that is offered; only the thought behind it really matters.

PART TWO:
UNFOLDING OF MY MINISTERIAL CAREER

Part Two of this book outlines my "multi-varied" denominational sojourn, and describes unique experiences in each of the 20 denominations that I have related to or interacted with in a formal capacity. I can honestly say that my experience in connection with each of them affected my spiritual growth in some way.

This section of the book is addressed to those readers who may have developed an interest in reading the background to the foregoing vignettes. I therefore offer a brief description of the varied denominational experiences that afforded me a fifty-year stint in the work of God. My story unfolds denomination by denomination.

DENOMINATION NO. 1: GOSPEL HALL (PLYMOUTH BRETHREN)

My earliest recollection of denominational functioning occurred at the age of six in the City of Trail, British Columbia, when my parents enrolled my older brother, David, and me in a Gospel Hall Sunday school. Of Mennonite extraction, and baptized in the General Conference Mennonite Church before they were married (baptism and church membership were a traditional Mennonite requirement for marriage), my parents virtually became denominational wanderers. My parents married during the Great Depression of 1929, and two years later migrated to British Columbia from Saskatchewan in search of employment. Rumours of job openings at the Canadian Mining and Smelting Company in Trail, BC, lured several Saskatchewan families to the City of Trail, and our family was one of them.

The trip from Waldheim, Saskatchewan to Trail, British Columbia was itself an awesome adventure because my parents depended on their big, old 1930 Buick truck to get them there. I later discovered the little known fact that the Buick division of General Motors *did* make trucks at one time. My parents' old Buick beast of burden featured very poor tires and bad mileage. In addition, Dad and Mom had insufficient funds to make the journey and hoped to find part-time work along the way. Oddly, the plan worked, my father taking on menial jobs at various locations across Saskatchewan, Alberta, and British Columbia. The trip to Trail, British Columbia, took several weeks to complete, upon arrival my father set up a makeshift tent, settled the family, and through the intercession of one of his Saskatchewan friends, who preceded our arrival, found employment as a bricklayer's helper with the Canadian Mining and Smelting Company.

One of George and Barbara Friesen's initial concerns, besides finalizing the matter of temporary housing, was the question of church affiliation. There was no Mennonite church of any kind nearby, so that was not an option. My parents accepted the suggestion of former acquaintances from Saskatchewan to attend a Plymouth Brethren congregation because they allegedly "believed a lot in Bible doctrine." The idea appealed to my parents, partly because they would be able to attend church with their friends. Soon we found ourselves worshipping in a tiny downtown church shaped like a little schoolhouse in the heart of the City of Trail. As I recall, about 35 people regularly attended "Gospel Hall" (as it was called), half of them children and teenagers. Sunday school classes for all ages were preceded by an early worship service the "Breaking of Bread" (also known as Holy Communion, or the Lord's Supper—depending on one's denominational affiliation). My parents did not attempt to participate in that ceremony since it was made known informally that this was a closed service; that is, it was open to only a select faithful few. We therefore attended Sunday school classes and the 11:00 a.m. worship service.

I should mention that Sunday school classes at the Gospel Hall were very small, but the elder who taught us was very keen for us to learn the names of the books of the Bible by heart as well as memorize a series of Bible verses. It was at the Gospel Hall that our family learned to sing short songs known as choruses. Basically, the text of each chorus was a Bible verse, often sung verbatim without much concern about rhyming the lines.

When it was time for the sermon to be delivered, one of two men stood up and "delivered the Word." I noticed that it was always the same two individuals who took this task upon themselves, and I was later informed that they were responding to the moving of the Holy Spirit. Even as a young boy I wondered why none of the other men who were present ever got moved by the Spirit, not that I expected my father to be one of them. After all, I was familiar with his behaviour at home and I did not consider him a holy man. I did worry, however, that I might not be so moved, should I fulfill my childhood dream and become a minister when I reached adulthood. Thirty years later, I discovered that the Plymouth Brethren practice had changed so much that congregations were now able to announce in the local Saturday paper who would be delivering the sermon the following day! It seems the Holy Spirit was now giving advance warning.

Trail Gospel Hall had a reputation for rigidity in every sphere, including the celebration of the Sacraments. Of course, they never used the word "Sacrament," but they did practice the Breaking of Bread. The ritual was part of an early service that took place before Sunday school, and was attended only by the very loyal. The later, 11:00 a.m. service was supposedly geared toward sinners and non-members. My father, who had a penchant for the unusual, liked to sit at the front of the church. After attending the Gospel Hall for some time, he decided it was time to take part in the early service as well. Our family sat in a pew near the front of the church, much to the consternation of the elders who were planning to celebrate the Breaking of Bread. Non-participants were allowed to observe the service, but they were expected to sit at the back of the church where they would not be served.

Although both of my parents considered themselves Christians and had been baptized and confirmed in the Mennonite Church in Saskatchewan, evidently the elders did not consider them worthy to participate in the ritual of the Lord's Supper. They therefore requested of my father that he and his family relocate themselves to the back of the church where the Lord's Supper would not be served. If memory serves correctly, we rose from our seats and left the church building, never to return to that church. Our four-year stint as Plymouth Brethren was over. A few years ago my wife and I made a trip to Trail only to discover that the congregation has long been since dissolved but the church building still stands and has since been remodeled into a family home.

Somehow, despite these experiences, restrictions, and disappointments, I have fond memories of those who so diligently taught us to respect and be very familiar with God's Holy Word.

Meaningful Moments in Ministry

DENOMINATION NO. 2: THE SALVATION ARMY

Over the next few years, our family undertook a wilderness wandering of church denominations, often attending different churches on Sundays for morning and evening services. In fact, while worshipping with our peers at the Gospel Hall, my brother, David, and I attended their Sunday school in the morning and stayed for the 11:00 a.m. morning service along with our parents. At that point our parents returned home and the two of us would remain in the city and attend an afternoon Sunday school class at the Salvation Army Hall. Our parents gave us funds to purchase lunch (a bowl of soup) at a local restaurant, and then head to the Salvation Army Hall located across the city for our second Sunday school class. A bowl of soup cost twenty-five cents in those days, but the experience of "eating out" made us feel like kings. After completing the class at the Salvation Army Hall, we walked the distance of a little more than a mile back to our home outside the city.

Before long, our family was very active in Salvation Army programs that included two Sunday worship services (morning and evening), Bible studies, and other activities. My older brother David, my two younger siblings, Norman and Nancy, and I, were dedicated to God in a formal service and became Junior Soldiers of the Salvation Army. Mom also enrolled David and I in a highly touted boys and girls choir whose leader required that boys wear black trousers, girls wear black skirts, and all wear white shirts. At this time, we made the acquaintance of the McColl-Gerard Trio which was made up of sisters Jean and Velma McColl and Bernice Gerard. I had difficulty understanding how Jean and Velma could be sisters since Velma was tall, thin, and somewhat shy, and Jean heavyset and confident and the main spokesperson for the group. Bernice later became an ordained Pentecostal minister and a successful radio and television preacher for many years—in fact, she carried on her ministry until she was well into her eighties.

When wanderlust again overtook my parents, we frequented a local Full Gospel Church and a Pentecostal Church. A few years later, when the McColl-Gerard Trio established a weekly radio program on radio station CJAT Trail, David and I sang duets on the show, accompanying ourselves respectively on guitar and banjo. Jean McColl held forth with the Gospel message even at a time when women ministers were a very rare phenomenon. Bernice continued this practice well into the 1990s, both in a local church as well as on her television program with Velma McColl. Bernice's television program was produced in Vancouver, British Columbia. Later, I frequently watched her television show out of admiration for her energy and as a form of reminiscence, I recently found a copy of her autobiography and a flood of very positive memories stirred in my mind.

By now, it was time to go to public school and I was quite fearful of the prospect. It helped that my older brother was already in school, and a few neighbour children were attending. It was a mile long walk to East Trail Elementary School, and by now I had learned enough of the English language to be able to relate to my peers at school. Within a very short time I learned to love school, especially the joy of receiving brightly colored stickers for doing good work. I learned how to write poetry, participated in a school choir and drama group, and endured endless name-calling because of my bright red hair and rather large ears. I shall not bore you with the creative labels my cruel peers came up with, but will leave those to your imagination.

Meaningful Moments in Ministry

DENOMINATION NO. 3: PRESBYTERIAN CHURCH IN CANADA

I was quite young during many of my parents' "wilderness wanderings," but I do recall attending services at three additional church congregations in Trail—Full Gospel, Pentecostal, and Presbyterian. In fact, our family attended every revival campaign in Trail, regardless of which church was sponsoring the event. My parents just could not get enough of religion; perhaps it was a reaction to their stoic Mennonite upbringing.

I recall that within a few weeks of trying it out, my parents decided that the Presbyterian Church was too formal for them and, besides, none of their Mennonite friends from Saskatchewan attended there. I recall that the church sanctuary was quite cold and bleak in appearance and atmosphere, and I made certain that my mother's hand was close at hand at all times.

DENOMINATION NO. 4: FULL GOSPEL CHURCH

Our time at the Full Gospel Church was also quite brief, although we did admire the singing/preaching style of a certain Reverend "Silliker." I recall that he presented every sentence he uttered with the same lilt and "melody." I decided then and there that if I was fortunate enough to enter the ministry in later life, I would preach in a more ordinary voice.

DENOMINATION NO. 5: PENTECOSTAL ASSEMBLIES OF CANADA

The Pentecostal church was a different matter and I have forgotten exactly what the attraction was for our affiliation with that congregation. As I recall, we attended there for about a year and during that time my brother, David, and I made it into the church orchestra. David played guitar and I played tenor banjo, something I still like to do. I even took 25 lessons on the tenor banjo at Ted Marr Studios in upper Trail. No doubt I would have continued the lessons if we had not relocated to rural Saskatchewan where we were unable to find a music teacher who knew anything about the tenor banjo. For that matter, there were no music teachers of any kind for miles around. Everyone in our neighbourhood played some kind of musical instrument, having learned to play entirely by experimentation!

Services at the Pentecostal church were lively and upbeat, and I quite enjoyed them. The music was particularly uplifting, and I can still recall the words of many of the songs we learned there. A difficulty arose for my parents in connection with evening services when the Holy Spirit apparently visited the congregation and almost everyone began speaking in tongues. This was a bit too much for my conservative Mennonite parents and they refused every invitation to join in. I recall a scene in which everyone was kneeling backwards into their pews, uttering strange sounds with which I was unfamiliar. A few individuals were literally crawling from one pew to the next, putting their arms around various parishioners, and praying with them in what I perceived to be unintelligible sounds. I was later told that this was a

"Holy Roller" Church, but it was also the last time we attended that particular church. It seems we were not "cut out" to be Holy Rollers, but I did enjoy their music!

DENOMINATION NO. 6: THE CHRISTIAN AND MISSIONARY ALLIANCE

Once again on the search for a church home in Trail, my parents followed some of their Mennonite friends from Saskatchewan in attending a new congregation of the Christian and Missionary Alliance denomination in Trail. Services were held in a remodeled storefront on the north side of the Columbia River in East Trail. This was the district in which my brother, David, and I attended elementary school. The pastor couple, Rev. and Mrs. Schroeder, were just starting out in the ministry and showed just the right amount of motivation and enthusiasm. Sensitivity, it turned out, was not Mrs. Schroeder's forte or else she had not taken a course on the subject in Bible College.

By this time, I was ten years old and I had gained considerable knowledge of Bible stories mostly by attending the Plymouth Brethren Sunday School and summer camp. I also had a healthy appetite to learn more about the Bible. Somehow, my brother and I managed to obtain a thick comic-type book of Bible stories, fully illustrated with pictures, and I literally devoured its contents. This knowledge did not go to waste.

One day I saw an ad in a church magazine advertising flannelgraph stories available from a company in Harrisburg, Pennsylvania, and for two dollars, I managed to order a set outlining several Old Testament accounts. When I received the lessons in the mail I was dying to do something with them, perhaps even teach a class some day, and I shared this dream with my mother. She spoke with the minister's wife, Mrs. Schroeder, who was responsible for the children's feature (lesson) during the morning worship service. The woman agreed to let me teach a lesson and I was immensely pleased. I studied hard, prepared my flannelgraph board, and arranged the figures in the order I was going to present them.

The lesson went well, and several people thanked me for my effort, but the event was very negatively overshadowed when Mrs. Schroeder summed up her opinion of the lesson by commenting to my mother, "Your son tried hard; I noticed that he has such big glasses; they look just like fish eyes on him."

Her words stung. Needless to say, it was my last flannelgraph lesson for a long time. The verse, "A word fitly spoken is like apples of gold in pictures of silver (Proverbs 25:11 KJV) comes to mind in this context. Fortunately, it was getting to be time for a major family move—back to Saskatchewan, so we now had a valid excuse to leave the Christian and Missionary Alliance Church.

I should mention one very positive experience with summer Daily Vacation Bible School (DVBS) with the Christian and Missionary Alliance Church. The event took place in the nearby community of Fruitvale, and my father was able to rent an abandoned storefront so the family could stay onsite. My mother, my three siblings and I, stayed in those quarters and attended Bible classes during the day. My father commuted to Trail to work and joined us for revival services in the evenings. An evangelist named Rev. Gordon Skitch was the preacher, and I was most impressed with his messages. Some forty years later, I chanced to meet his son in Calgary and we shared a few happy memories of his father's ministry.

My most impressive experience in DVBS was the handiwork opportunity. Each camper was given a small piece of plywood, about the size of a Bible with which to make a wall plaque. The plywood was coated with several layers of shellac, and while the shellac was still sticky, we fixed letters of macaroni to the plaque spelling out short Bible verses. I was amazed that such small pieces of food could be used to enlighten onlookers with the contents of the Word of God and I treasured mine for many years.

The year was 1946, and my father's health began deteriorating. His lungs were filled with residue from the contaminated air he was breathing in the smelter environment. As I look back, it is hard to believe that he went on to live to be almost 94 years old. Dad's doctor told him to leave his employ with the Canadian and Mining Smelting Company and head for the open country, perhaps move to the prairies. My parents eagerly heeded the pull of their upbringing and migrated back to Saskatchewan, the land of their birth.

My father traded a 1929 Model A Ford car and $25.00 for a quarter section of land near Duck Lake, Saskatchewan, sight unseen, and when we arrived, we were expected suddenly to become farmers. My brother and I knew nothing of horses, harnesses, plows, or milking, but we soon learned. My parents were able to procure a team of horses, several cows and chickens, and a few pieces of aging farm equipment. Our hopes were high; we were surely going to make a go of it as farmers.

We made the trip to Saskatchewan by automobile in three days, having shipped our household goods by railway car. Dad leased an entire railroad car and we filled it with everything we could cram into it—furniture, tools, household items, clothing, and other "precious" items. When we arrived at our destination we settled in an abandoned log house on the land Dad had purchased. Our shipped goods, however, were nowhere to be found, so we had to borrow a modest range of items from nearby relatives. It took three months to locate the goods we shipped since someone had accidentally rolled the freight car containing our family goods onto an abandoned railway line near Shellbrook, Saskatchewan, some 30 miles (48 kilometres) away. The railway office seemed to have no record of having brought the railcar to Saskatchewan, and thus we had virtually no supplies to assist us in adjusting to rural life.

One day a railway employee spotted an abandoned railway car on an unused line and notified the head office. The railroad car contained virtually all of our worldly possessions. It was in this manner that we were finally able to obtain our goods and properly set up house. In the meantime, my parents set about finding a suitable church home for the family.

Meaningful Moments in Ministry

DENOMINATION NO. 7: SEVENTH-DAY ADVENTIST CHURCH IN CANADA

Our family's sojourn into the religious realm back in Saskatchewan was not immediately satisfying. The local church we first chose was Mennonite, directly connected to my parents' ethnic roots. However, having bitten into the evangelical/fundamentalist sector of Christianity while living in Trail, my parents found that the theology and practices of the Mennonite church they had left behind a decade earlier somewhat stifling and lack lustre. They wanted something with "more life," less staid, and with less emphasis on ethnicity.

About this time a neighbouring lay preacher of the Seventh Day Adventist Church offered to hold Bible studies in our home, complete with slides of the Holy Land, and our parents thought this might be an enjoyable way to spend winter evenings. Now in our early teens, my brother and I thought this was particularly good idea since the lay preacher's daughter was our age and quite pleasant to look at. Thanks to the lay preacher's influence, I enrolled in a two-year correspondence course with the Seventh Day Adventist Church, but ceased taking lessons when I felt that pressure was being exerted on me to recognize Saturday as the Lord's Day instead of Sunday.

Having read and put to heart the meaning of Romans 14:5 (NIV), "One person considers one day more sacred than another; another considers every day alike. Each of them should be fully convinced in their own mind," I couldn't really get excited about what I perceived to be an extraordinary emphasis on Saturday as the Divinely-prescribed Sabbath Day. After all, I reasoned, many Christians who had worshipped on Sunday for so many centuries couldn't be wrong! However, I did receive a certificate of graduation from the course even though I did not make the commitment to honour Saturday as the Christian Holy Day.

In the meantime, the Seventh Day Adventist home classes were going well, and the lectures delivered by the lay preacher were interesting. At times some of our neighbours dropped in to take part in the evening's program. After a few months, I noticed that things began to change, and the lay preacher announced that the lessons had been arranged to lead up to the truth that Saturday was the proper day for worship, not Sunday. My father refused to accept this "truth," and an argument ensued. Finally, the lay preacher's wife, who was quite outspoken, confronted my father.

"Mr. Friesen, "she said, "If you would get down on your knees right now and pray, I know that God would reveal this truth to you." At that point, our guests were asked to leave, much to the disappointment of my brother and myself. There were even a few days when we thought about the possibility of enrolling in a Seventh Day high school in Alberta that our guest had mentioned several times. Obviously, this never happened.

Meaningful Moments in Ministry

DENOMINATION NO. 8: ANGLICAN CHURCH OF CANADA

After this particular set of unfortunate developments, our family continued to look for a fulfilling place to worship and visited the local Anglican Church a few times. It was there that we were introduced to what we perceived to be very a formal order of worship (without Latin), and hot cross buns at Easter time! However, our visits were not entirely in vain. Through our interactions with this congregation, I discovered and quickly enrolled in and completed a correspondence Bible course with the Anglican Church of Canada. I was quite disappointed not to receive a certificate from the correspondence school, although I do remember finishing the course. Perhaps they did not issue certificates of completion. Imagine how disappointing this was to a young teen who wanted in a formal manner to learn as much about the Bible as he could.

DENOMINATION NO. 9: WILLIAM ABERHART'S INDEPENDENT BAPTIST CHURCH

While my family cast about for a new church home our family continued sporadically to frequent the Mennonite Church and my parents continued to tell their relatives about the good times they had experienced in the evangelical community back in Trail. I am sure that our relatives must have thought them a bit strange, critical and even a bit too judgmental. My own spiritual journey continued by enrolling in a Bible studies course with the *Calgary Prophetic Bible Institute* begun by Alberta Premier William Aberhart and later affiliated with the Independent Baptist Churches of Alberta. When I finished the course I was awarded a certificate of completion, and I was very proud of that achievement.

The course was a basic introduction to the Bible with no particular emphasis on selective doctrinal themes. I later learned that Mr. Aberhart did hold to some very definite ideas on salvation, sanctification, and eschatology, but none of these were unduly emphasized in the course I took. As I look back on the experience, I have to admire this approach because the originators of the course appear to have been more interested in spreading the Gospel than promoting particular doctrinal beliefs.

The above events took place during my early teens, those impressionable years when young people are seriously involved in framing their own parameters of belief. Sometimes I wonder if I have deviated very much from the behaviour I viewed, the information I processed, and the models I confronted.

DENOMINATION NO. 10: THE CHURCH OF GOD (ANDERSON, INDIANA)

One day word reached our community about a promising church congregation across the North Saskatchewan River. It was a Church of God congregation, with denominational ties to headquarters in Anderson, Indiana.

The Silvergrove Church of God was made up of several former Lutheran families who left that church after having been influenced by a travelling evangelist who had visited the area some years earlier. The main beliefs of the church appealed to my parents—salvation by faith alone, baptism by immersion, amillennialism as an eschatological stance, and a strong emphasis on evangelism. After a few visits to the church, my parents decided that the minister *did* preach the true Gospel, and the lively hymn singing proved to be another strong drawing card. It is important to note that while there are a number of denominations using the phrase "Church of God," the Anderson group considers itself solidly evangelically orthodox. One of their distinguishing features is that they do not believe in formal church membership, a minor regulation that kept me from preaching in one of their churches in Kansas a few years later. I will describe this experience in more detail in a later section.

Having discussed the matter with several families of relatives who were also looking for something new, our family participated in what turned out to be a very enriching experience at the Silvergrove Church of God. Every Sunday several Mennonite families crossed the North Saskatchewan River by ferry and headed to the Church of God. The arrival of new families doubled the attendance of the church and no doubt, the pastor was delighted to witness the sudden growth. Perhaps there was also hope that the newcomers might add financial assistance to church coffers.

Attending the Church of God meant a weekly ferryboat ride across the North Saskatchewan River, and sometimes weather conditions did not permit the ferry to operate. Many times, high winds, shifting sandbars, or faulty equipment kept the boat ashore and when we arrived at the dock, we found we had to turn back home. At this time, we were using a 1929 Model A Ford as a family car, with one major defect. The brakes did not work. This did not deter my father from negotiating the old car down a steep winding road to the ferry landing. Dad's solution was merely to shift the car into reverse gear at the top of the hill, and let the car coast down the hill toward the ferry. If the car went too fast, dad would gun the motor and slowly let out the clutch, thereby using the transmission as a brake! When I think back, it was a miracle that Dad was always able to stop the car as it approached the far end of the ferry. The water at that end of the ferry was at least 20 feet (6.5 metres) deep and had the car broken through the dubious-looking chain at the end of the ferry, we would all surely have drowned!

Fellowship in the Church of God was spiritually fulfilling. We had a vibrant youth group, where each of us was given an opportunity for "pulpit time." We were encouraged to present special music (solos, duets, trios, or even quartets), lead hymn singing, share a testimony, or read from the scriptures. Undoubtedly this experience helped fuel my desire to enter the ministry. Within two or three years of fellowship with the congregation, it seemed appropriate to enter into baptism (by immersion) as a symbol of having adopted the Christian faith. One Sunday, my brother David, my cousin, Elmer Reimer, and I, joined a few others in stepping into the cold waters of the North Saskatchewan River and being baptized by the late Rev. Ludwig Hoffman.

Fellowship with the Church of God provided me with many happy memories. We learned to sing boisterous Gospel songs and attend annual revival meetings held in a large tent. Even though we were teenagers, we were given regular opportunities to participate in various aspects of the formal worship service.

DENOMINATION NO. 11: MENNONITE CHURCH CANADA (FORMERLY, GENERAL CONFERENCE MENNONITE CHURCH)

In the meantime, when the ferry was not operating, our family continued to attend the local Mennonite church, particularly their monthly youth fest, an evening service designed to encourage young people to participate in healthy forms of social interaction.

The nature of Saskatchewan weather often dictated the regularity of our attendance at the Church of God. The roads were usually impassable during spring ice break and in fall when the ferry was removed from the river for winter storage, we had to wait several weeks for the river to freeze over so we could navigate over the ice on the way to church. On Sundays when we were unable to make the trip, we usually attended the local General Conference Mennonite Church congregation. When we learned that the local Mennonite minister was offering catechetical classes for young people, David and I immediately signed up. We were pretty well prepared to do anything to be with our peers, and as a bonus, the class also proved to be quite informative.

I have fond memories of fellowship with the Church of God and lived through the period of transition the congregation experienced when they switched from use of the German language to English. The initial plan was to have one Sunday service a month in English, then two a month, and then change to English altogether. I recall the Sunday it was announced that no more services would be held in the German language. One older gentleman, an elder who used to sit on one of the front pews, got up and made a great show of walking out of the church, his heels thumping loudly on the hardwood floor. We never saw him in church again, that is, until the day of his funeral several years later. The incident made a great impression on my teen age mind; I resolved never to be too adamant about matters that I was sure would not significantly affect the Kingdom of God.

After moving to the City of Saskatoon, Saskatchewan, a few years later I recall being scheduled to preach in the local Church of God in both the morning and evening services the day my oldest son, Bruce, was born. Many years later, I presided at the Calgary wedding of the daughter of a friend who had been our youth sponsor at the Silvergrove Church of God. Concerned somewhat about to keeping contact with the denomination of my baptism when I studied in Kansas, I contacted the local church superintendent to inquire as to the availability of a student pastorate. By then, I had completed five years of theological studies and preached many times in a variety of churches. When I told the superintendent that I had taken formal membership in another denomination since my baptism with the Church of God, he discouraged me from going any further with my application. He reminded me that the Church of God did not believe in formal church membership, a fact that I knew, but did not comprehend just how important this belief was. I therefore cast about for another opportunity for pastoral service. In 2009 my wife and I happened to visit the little town where this particular church was located and found it abandoned and looking somewhat dilapidated.

Meaningful Moments in Ministry

DENOMINATION NO. 12: THE MENNONITE BRETHREN CHURCH

One summer day in 1954 my father took ill with double pneumonia and David and I rushed him to Rosthern Hospital some 35 miles (56 kilometres) away. Placing his stethoscope on my father's chest, the doctor took a long look at him, and told us to take him to the city hospital in Saskatoon as fast as we could. "There is nothing I can do for him here," the doctor observed. The physicians who examined Dad in Saskatoon gave him 24 hours to live because by now he had also caught pleurisy. My brother and I conferred and he drove the car home to take care things at the farm while I looked after Dad.

I decided to stay in the city to be near Dad and obtain employment so I could send money home. I was expected to send money home, of course, because my father believed that until we were twenty-one years of age, half of any money we earned belonged in family coffers. I dutifully fulfilled this mandate and my contributions assisted in meeting several financial commitments for farm obligations. About ten years later, my father informed me that I was the only one of his five children to ever fulfill this requirement and he returned all my money to me. I was a student at the time with my own family obligations, and I was very glad for the support!

In Saskatoon I found rooming through some friends for $25.00 a month, and walked the streets of Saskatoon for seven days looking for work. Every evening I would visit my father in hospital and by the end of the week, the Lord intervened and gave me a job as a ditch digger with the City of Saskatoon Engineering Department. I held that job for six summers; it was always waiting for me at the end of each college year in spring.

In fall, 1954, it was my intention to enroll in a Bible College, preferably the Camrose Bible Institute in Camrose, Alberta, affiliated with the Church of God. Meanwhile, my cousin, Mervin Reimer, with whom I roomed in Saskatoon during the summer months, encouraged me to join him at Bethany Bible Institute (now called Bethany College), in Hepburn, Saskatchewan, where he was already a student. The school is affiliated with the Mennonite Brethren Conference of Saskatchewan. I readily yielded to my cousin's invitation partly because he offered to fill in my registration form and partly because the cost of tuition was slightly lower than it was at the Camrose school.

Sometimes I wonder if I made the right decision.

Life at Bethany Bible Institute was an eye-opener. This was the fifties, the years during which Rock Hudson and Doris Day dominated the first television set I had ever seen. Elvis Presley was also doing his thing before a large television audience on the Ed Sullivan Show. Men in the know were wearing pink shirts and charcoal colored pants and sometimes even matching underwear! These developments had little effect on life at Bethany, and when the local town theatre played the movie, *The Yearling*, we were forbidden to attend. We were told, "It would not be a good testimony for the town if Bible College students were seen at such a 'worldly' event!"

During my first year at Bethany, I roomed with my cousin who introduced me to the vicissitudes of dormitory life and the challenges of living with a roommate. I enjoyed my classes, and thanks to the encouragement and example of my peers, for the first time in my life I learned how to study. Several college staff motivated me to write departmental examinations for high school subjects I was still lacking, so that by the time I graduated from Bethany with a Diploma in Religious Education, I also completed enough grade twelve subjects to qualify for admittance to my next college.

My two favourite subjects at Bethany were homiletics, and Bible customs and manners. When I gave my maiden sermon in homiletics class and achieved an "A" grade from the instructor, the late Rev. Jake Epp, I knew the Lord was confirming my calling for me. The course on Bible customs and manners gave me a new way to understand the scriptures, and I hoped some day to visit the Holy Land. My Bethany College instructor lecturing on Bible customs emphasized that the study of varying cultural arrangements should help one realize that different cultures hold to beliefs and customs unique to them. This eye-opening course made it so much more possible to understand difficult passages in the Bible. No doubt the experience also motivated me later to research, visit, and write about such communities as Amish, Chinese Canadians, French Canadians, Doukhobors, First Nations, Métis, and Sikhs. I achieved my goal to visit the Holy Land in 1980.

The majority of students at Bethany Bible Institute had Mennonite Brethren background and was very loyal to their cultural connection. I saw them as non-questioning conformists—obedient, quiet, unimaginative, and somewhat self-righteous. Many members of the faith continued to celebrate the fact that the denomination had severed its ties with its parent body, the General Conference Mennonite Church, on January 6, 1860, while in Russia. The issue motivating the division was worldliness; apparently, the parent body had backslidden. It is to the credit of both denominations that a few decades ago they were able to cooperate in the merger of two Bible Colleges located in Langley, British Columbia to form Columbia Bible College.

Despite the conservative tendencies of the denomination that sponsored Bethany College, the school's students often played tricks on one another in the dormitories, and even disobeyed minor school rules. The night before my class graduated, several graduating peers and myself snuck out of the dormitory after midnight and built a huge bonfire in a neighbouring farmer's field so we could have a late night (early morning) wiener roast. *That*, in my day, was analogous to open rebellion!

I took singing lessons at Bethany College from an instructor named

Albert Lepp who, in my estimation, sounded much like the late Italian tenor, Mario Lanza! To my surprise, in midwinter Mr. Lepp invited me to sing in a male octet that performed at the annual Saskatoon Oratorio Festival. When spring arrived it was also time to participate in the local annual spring concert, but I developed a cold and told Mr. Lepp that my voice would crack if I performed. Still, he insisted that I deliver my solo, assuring me that I would hit the high notes in fine shape. As I expected, I did not reach that note.

The selection I was to sing was entitled, "When God is Near," with the words to the chorus being, "When God is near, my heart is filled with ecstasy." The word "ecstasy" was sung to a high "E" note, and, you guessed it, my voice cracked in the middle of the note and the audience broke up with laughter! Needless to say, it was the last public concert I ever performed in solo. Is there any chance that I might get over it?

After nearly three years at Bethany, I received membership in the Mennonite Brethren Church in Saskatoon and continued working for the City of Saskatoon. When I completed the sought-after Diploma in Religious Education I was eager to move on to another college and did so, this time to Winnipeg, Manitoba where another Mennonite Brethren institution was located. Now known as Canadian Mennonite University, the Mennonite Brethren Bible College (MBBC) offered several undergraduate degrees, with some courses accredited by Waterloo University in Ontario, as well as Tabor College in Kansas—another Mennonite Brethren institution.

I completed a Bachelor of Religious Education Degree at the Mennonite Brethren Bible College in Winnipeg. The college gave me one year of credit for my work at Bethany College and I was able to complete the program in two years. During my stay in Winnipeg I worked at a lumberyard, pulled squeegees across a film at a poster-making business called *Display Industries*, and did odd jobs, following up on want ads in the local newspaper. Some of my earnings were assigned toward an installment plan of six dollars a month to pay for a portable, non-electric typewriter. It served me for many years and I was only able to share its virtues with an unsuspecting party in 2001. It was still in working order when I gave it away.

In Winnipeg, I found it difficult to work nights and still stay awake during classes the next morning, but somehow I managed. I discovered that the more hours I worked each week, the lower my grades slipped. Several colleagues and I were asked to take turns preaching at a local Mennonite church and the pay was six dollars a Sunday. I was happy to have the opportunity to engage in some form of ministry, but at that point, I did not think of myself as good enough to be paid for preaching and told my peers that I would refuse the money. I immediately was brought up short by one of my peers who scolded me for attempting to spoil the church.

"They *need* to pay for your ministry," he said. "If you do not take pay for your services you will teach the congregation that ministers can live without pay. You may not need the money, but the rest of us do, so take it and don't make the rest of us look bad."

I assured my colleague that I *did* need the money, but I was not sure I was qualified to be paid for preaching. However, I soon adjusted, realizing that it took me many hours of study to prepare a sermon. College life for someone with limited funds and no access to student loans is difficult. It was difficult putting in as many as forty hours a week at work, and still maintain some semblance of decent grades.

As graduation neared at MBBC, I made plans to study further either at Waterloo University in Ontario, or Tabor College in Kansas. At that point, the president of MBBC approached me about assuming a pastorate but I told him I wanted to study further. He seemed surprised, and said something about not perceiving me as a scholar, but rather as a pastor. It later occurred to me that his judgment was a bit off because later I managed to do both. It is always enlightening to discover what people *really* think about you, but perhaps sometimes it is better not to know.

My next move was to Tabor College in Kansas, another Mennonite

Brethren institution, and here I eventually attained a Bachelor of Arts Degree in sociology.

After a semester of study at Tabor College I returned to Canada for the summer months to work at Camp Arness, located a two-hour drive north of Winnipeg. My responsibilities included arriving a few weeks early to help prepare the camp. Then, every ten days a new group of teenaged boys arrived and became my personal charges. I presented daily devotional talks at chapel for the camp, supervised a boy's cabin, and tried to spend some time with my family. Two of my worst memories a bout Camp Arness were the early morning dip in Lake Winnipeg, and fish flies.

Lake Winnipeg is a very large body of water, or should I say "cold water," and is about 250 miles (402 kilometres) long and about one-third that wide. Still, during a storm it can feature waves that are nearly 15 feet (four metres) high. Imagine trying to wade into the lake in such condition at 6 a.m. for a morning dip. Looking back, I don't think the boys even enjoyed it all that much, but it was a camp rule and an alternative to a cold shower from a huge pail strapped to a tall tree.

Fish flies are a staple to Lake Winnipeg. Sometime in late summer, the entire lake turns pea soup green. The larvae linger on top of the lake in a thick layer, so one can almost walk on the water. The larvae then transform into swarms of fish flies that migrate as fast as they can to any lit light bulb. They then gather around the light, forming huge clumps almost a foot (30 centimetres) thick. After they die, the entire campground smells like dead fish. It becomes the responsibility of camp staff to grab shovels and commence a quick burial procedure.

Despite the encounter with fish flies, working at the boys' camp was very rewarding. I enjoyed conducting daily devotions with my charges in my cabin, and put a lot of energy into preparing biographies of missionaries to relate in morning chapel. Later I edited my notes and witnessed the publication of many of these biographies in issues of the *Mennonite Brethren Herald*.

Another related memory takes us back to the Steinreich Mennonite

Brethren Church in Kansas. Our first three children were born before I graduated from Tabor College, and the oldest, Bruce Kelly, was only three years old, Karen Barbara was two years old and Gaylene Joan was a newborn. Since the church, where I was pastor, was too small to have a nursery, so Bruce was elected to accompany me on the platform. He was cautioned to sit very still and not distract the congregation, particularly while I was preaching. To his credit, I can say that he exercised excellent platform behaviour without receiving anything more than a warning. Perhaps this is why he later entered the ministry for a while; he must have enjoyed his platform experience. He is currently a professor of sociology at Tampa University in Florida.

Watching how some people's children behave in church today, I often wonder what they are told about the house of God. Is it still a place of awe and worship like it was in my day?

DENOMINATION NO. 13: THE BAPTIST UNION

Parenthetically, I should mention that one summer in Winnipeg I was invited to be a relief preacher at three small Baptist Union congregations. I already had a summer job loading and unloading railway cars bulging with bales of heavy lumber, and the pay was good, but the lure to preaching continued. My colleague in this somewhat dreary, unfulfilling occupation of handling heavy lumber was a young Baptist fellow named Jack Chatwin.

When Jack discovered that I was a Bible College student, he told his pastor who just happened to be in need of a summer replacement. Then, at the invitation of none other than the late Reverend Leslie Tarr, I worked as a summer relief preacher for three Baptist congregations in Winnipeg—and I took the pay! I greatly enjoyed this experience, and had I spent much more time with Reverend Tarr, there is a good chance I might have become a Baptist!

DENOMINATION NO. 14: THE EVANGELICAL UNITED BRETHREN CHURCH

During the sixties, many graduates of Tabor College transferred to Emporia State University for graduate work because that institution readily accepted Tabor credits even though Tabor had not yet obtained full accreditation. Emporia State University is world renown because Emporia is also the site of its famous *Emporia Gazette*, made famous by the late William Allen White. White, it was said, won the Pulitzer Prize for an editorial not more than three sentences in length.

I followed some of my fellow Tabor classmates to Emporia, enrolling in a Master of Science degree program in sociology and anthropology. Because of distance factors, I maintained my Mennonite Brethren country pastorate in Marion, usually driving 60 miles (96 kilometres) to school three times a week.

As I prepared to leave Tabor College, an older member of the church approached me and asked me what my future plans were. I told him I was off to do graduate work and ultimately work toward getting a doctorate.

"Why do you want a doctorate?" my mentor inquired, and I glibly answered, "I like studying."

"That is all very well," he went on, "and you no doubt have the ability to undertake this, but is the brotherhood ready for that? Will the community be able to benefit from your extra learning?"

Naturally, I asked him what he meant by that statement, and he went on to explain that our gifts and talents are not ours to hone; they belong to the community. If I were to obtain a doctorate, how would it value the brotherhood?

At first, I did not like what I was hearing, even though I knew that the undercurrents of my would-be mentor's words were true. I have often thought about them since, and sometimes passed them along to my own students. It is thoughts like these—defining moments—we call them, that often seem to come up at just the right time, bring us up short, and make us think. They force us to examine our motives and reason for being. In the meantime, I was off to study for a master's degree.

The highlight of studies at Emporia State University was working with the late Professor Roy Durham, who was my advisor. He had a tremendous sense of humour and was always an interesting speaker. It is because of his influence and that of the late Dr. Ernest E. Bayles, my Ph.D. advisor at the University of Kansas, that I resolved to provide the same kind and supportive treatment to my own graduate students.

Professor Durham used to like to tell stories and poke mild fun at society. He worried about the extra weight Americans were putting on long before it was popular to do so. He claimed that the average size of uniform for American troops increased by two sizes between World War I and World War II. As an usher in the local Methodist Church, he also claimed that he used to fit six people into a church pew but now only five would fit and that was with the aid of a long ushers' paddle to leverage them in!

One of Professor Durham's favourite stories, and I heard it more than once since I took several courses with him, had to do with gradual change. It seemed that an oil company had discovered oil on land owned by an elderly couple near Eureka, Kansas. The old couple suddenly had riches beyond their wildest dreams. Not willing to be stingy with their new resources, one day as the old farmer was preparing to go to town and do a little spending, he asked his wife if there was anything special she wanted from town. After all, they could afford it. Today we would say, "They were rollin' in it!"

The woman is said to have thought about her husband's offer for a bit, and then with her eyes wide open in wonderment and eager anticipation replied, "Could you bring me a new axe?" No doubt, most of us would have asked for a new car, an expensive vacation, or even a jet plane! To this Kansas woman, however, a new axe was a real luxury!

When my program of studies at Emporia State University was completed, I moved to the University of Kansas located at Lawrence, Kansas, to pursue a doctorate. Although I did qualify to earn a part-time salary as a graduate assistant, I needed to find other work to supplement the meager pay. After all, I had a family of four to support. Within weeks of arriving in Lawrence, a fellow graduate student informed me that several students with Mennonite background had been invited to assume rural pastorates with the Evangelical United Brethren (EUB) Church that was experiencing a shortage of ministers. I liked the idea, and made arrangements to meet with the local superintendent, Rev. Henry Vogel, since he had had previous experience with Mennonite ministerial students, he was delighted to receive my application and soon assigned me to a rural charge.

Shortly thereafter, I found myself pastor of two tiny congregations at Corning, Kansas (The Corning and New Eden congregations), located just four miles (six kilometres) apart, but 90 miles (145 kilometres) from home. The result was that I had to make a long trip by car each weekend, but both congregations were very receptive. Although I was driving an old car, I was never late for church, but noticed that a family who lived across the street was consistently late. They seemed to wait for the first hymn to be sung before they left their front steps.

Ministering to an EUB Church was a bit different in some ways. For example, this was the first time anyone had ever called me "The Reverend," but I gradually got used to it. There was a lot of respect for the ministerial office in that parish. At Corning, I studied EUB history and doctrine, and discovered that the denomination was a 1946 merger of two similar denominations, the former Evangelical Association and the former United Brethren Church, the latter even having some Mennonite roots. Perhaps that is why I immediately felt at home in the EUB church. At Corning I also picked up a great deal of informal Kansas history and conducted my first baptism. As an indication of the tenacity and loyalty of rural life in Kansas, one farmer informed me that he and his wife were sleeping in the very bed in which he was born!

After serving the Corning-New Eden charge for just one year, the superintendent assigned me to Camp Creek EUB Church located only 60 miles (96 kilometres) from the University of Kansas where I was still a student. Two years later he found another charge made up of the Stull and Big Springs congregations only 12 miles (19 kilometres) from Kansas University. In the meantime, a professor from Evangelical Theological Seminary in Naperville, Illinois, made weekly trips to Topeka, Kansas to deliver a course on contemporary theology to EUB ministers. Always an eager student, I enrolled in the course, and met a number of ministers from neighbouring EUB churches. It was the third time I had taken a course in contemporary theology (at three different institutions), but I always found the content challenging. The following year I enrolled in a similar course at the Kansas School of Religion, wrote a paper on the great theologian, Karl Barth, and got an "A" for my efforts.

Section One of this book contains several stories of my sojourn at Camp Creek EUB Church so I shall let them comprise a summery of my ministry there.

The Stull and Big Springs congregations were quite close in distance but had escaped the inclinations toward merger when the EUBs joined the United Methodists in 1968. Although much smaller in congregational numbers today, they still practice some of their historical denominational ways. Part of the reason they prefer to remain independent of each other is because they originated from quite different traditions. The Big Springs congregation, for example, was a former United Brethren Church while the Stull congregation was formerly part of the Evangelical Association.

It took me less than fifteen minutes to drive from the Stull Church to Big Springs on Sunday mornings, and my first service was at Stull. If it meant being on time for the Big Springs service, I could never preach overtime. The same held true for youth group meetings in Sunday nights. My successor had the times reversed at the suggestion of the Stull Church. The congregation said that it was their turn to have an opportunity to meet with the minister after church and they could never do this if he or she left for Big Springs immediately after the Benediction.

In the "olden days" churches did not have air conditioning, and few country churches today have that privilege. Thus in the hot summer days with the temperature around 90 degrees Fahrenheit (32 degrees Celsius) and plenty of humidity, a church can get quite uncomfortable. Some of the men at Stull said that my wearing a suit coat during the summer made them uncomfortable and would I please preach in my shirtsleeves. I did so, but always donned my jacket for services at Big Springs! I was present for the first service that my successor conducted and I noticed that he wore a black robe over his shirt. I wondered how long it would take the men of the church get to him to eliminate the robe!

It was at the Stull Church that I became a music teacher! Although I knew a number of chords on my old Spanish guitar, I hardly considered myself a virtuoso at any level. One day a woman at Stull Church heard me strumming and decided that I give teach her son guitar lessons. I did not particularly relish the idea since I only played by ear and hardly even knew the names of the chords I was using. Nevertheless, I let myself be talked into it and word got around that the preacher was offering guitar lessons. I quickly bought some guitar books, brushed up on the names of the chords I was using, and soon I had four students. Sadly, only one of them, a young married woman of about thirty, did any practicing. The other three students were teenage boys who either soon dropped out or cried at lessons because they were showing themselves up for not practicing. This worried me some; did the congregation expect that I would naturally be *successful* at teaching guitar? Within a year, the young woman in question was playing guitar as well as I was and I was happy to stop giving lessons. By this time, my program of studies for the Ph.D. was completed, and it was time to move back to Canada.

While studying at the University of Kansas, I spent two years working a graduate assistant and was assigned to the university's reading laboratory. There I met a fellow student and fellow worker named Bill Antoine, a retired sailor who was studying to become a teacher. The fact that Bill was a devoted Roman Catholic seemed to make little difference to our relationship; Bill and I hit it off at once. Although we had very different backgrounds, and subsequently varying ideas about life, we discovered that we could talk openly about virtually any subject and still respect one another's opinions. That, in my estimation, is a rare privilege, not often granted in life. As part-time employees, we were assigned to work in the university reading laboratory, helping students attain better study habits. Among other things, Bill and I taught speed-reading and designed a test to help students determine their reading speed and comprehension. I discovered that the reading lab used our test for many years afterward. Bill and I spent time outside of class hours with our families and corresponded for a long time after graduation. I can still remember the empty feeling I had in entering the reading laboratory after Bill had left campus for a job in Florida. I really missed him.

Meaningful Moments in Ministry

DENOMINATION NO. 15: THE UNITED METHODIST CHURCH

As I mentioned earlier, in 1968 the Evangelical United Brethren Church and the Methodist Church of America merged to form the United Methodist Church of America. I became a United Methodist minister overnight because of the merger, but it made little difference to my theology. Doctrinally, there were no basic differences between the EUBs and the Methodists, so only a little adjustment in church structure was necessary for the merger to take place. Unfortunately, after the merger church officials decided to close down a number of rural churches where there was duplication of facilities, often to the detriment of church attendance. Many rural families did not want their church closed even if a parallel facility was close by, so instead of yielding to official action, many of them simply left the church. Once the folks at church headquarters back east caught on to their miscalculation, they stopped closing down country churches.

As merger talks got underway, a number of dissident congregations banded together to resist. In eastern Canada, the EUBs joined with the United Church of Canada, but two conferences, the Northwest conference in Oregon, Washington, and other nearby states, and the western Canadian conference opted out of the merger and formed an independent denomination known as The Evangelical Church in North America. Later the Canadian faction merged with the Missionary Church to become the Evangelical Missionary Church.

By this time, I had completed my Ph.D. Degree and according to the requirements of my student visa, had to move back to Canada. At this time, I also obtained a position as Assistant Professor in the

Faculty of Education at the University of Calgary, and my ministerial credentials were transferred to the Evangelical Church in Alberta.

Meaningful Moments in Ministry

DENOMINATION NO. 16: THE EVANGELICAL CHURCH IN CANADA

After returning to Canada it seemed appropriate to affiliate with the Canadian counterpart of the former EUB church, now known as the Evangelical Church in Canada. We aligned ourselves with Centre Street Evangelical Church in Calgary where I taught Sunday school, preached occasionally, and took part in a number of other church activities. A year later, however, I was invited to be minister of a new independent, interfaith church in our neighbourhood and I accepted the position. The newly established independent group adopted the name, Huntington Hills Community Church (HHCC), and I served there for twelve years. After that, I took a year's sabbatical leave from the University of Calgary, and on returning to Calgary, returned to the Centre Street Church. In 1980 I served Centre Street Church as interim pastor for nine months before their present minister, the Reverend Henry Shore, arrived.

I was minister of Huntington Hills Community Church from 1968 to 1980, and the experience proved to be a highlight of my ministerial career. A true community church, HHCC attracted a wide range of religious backgrounds. Its format mainly appealed to families of mixed denominational backgrounds. For example, if a Lutheran was married to a Roman Catholic, or if a Methodist was married to a Baptist, they felt quite at home in the church. We tried to honour and respect all Christian church traditions. The church never sought to gain legal status as a denomination, but maintained informal ties to several denominations. During this time, it was for my benefit that the

Evangelical Church graciously maintained my ministerial credentials.

Huntington Hills Community Church (HHCC) never built a building, but held services in a Roman Catholic school, and later in a community building. The concept was that a wider appeal could best be forthcoming if a more neutral site was used for church activities. Within three years of its origin, the congregation grew to include 300 people of diverse denominational backgrounds.

HHCC was a product of the experimental sixties, and our worship services reflected this. While elected members conducted church board meetings, any member of the congregation could attend the meetings and everyone present had a vote. This freedom led to all kinds of innovations including worship services that highlighted monthly experiments such as running a service backwards (starting with the Benediction), so that latecomers could find out what usually went on before the arrived at church!

As I mentioned earlier, one Sunday morning service consisted of the playing of "Jesus Christ Superstar," by a local radio station when the musical first originated, then interviewing listeners as to their opinions on it. Another idea was to put slips of paper into various hymnals at random and have recipient worshippers provide the various parts of the service. As I recall, the minister got stuck with the sermon!

The experimental approach of HHCC was in keeping with the restless spirit of the sixties, with every major denomination struggling to keep their members interested. During the decade, few church buildings were built in Calgary, and newly established fellowships used schools and community centers to get started. Those were interesting times.

At the height of its operation in the seventies, Huntington Hills Community Church sponsored the largest Boy Scout Troop in the City of Calgary, and also worked with the Girl Guide Movement. Each year we held a joint worship service with the local Roman Catholic Church that served as sponsor for the local Girl Guide chapter. These were the sixties when every facet of institutional life was under fire. However, because of the actions of some ecumenically minded individuals, they were also times when some unusual cooperative ventures were undertaken. Many of us from different denominational backgrounds learned a great deal about each other during that decade.

In 1981 my son, Bruce, moved to Calgary to pursue graduate studies at the University of Calgary, having completed his undergraduate work at the University of Waterloo. We contacted the superintendent of the Evangelical Church and were given authorization to establish a branch church in the Forest Lawn district of Calgary. This arrangement continued for four years. The folks at Centre Street Church were not too excited about setting up a branch church and offered no financial support for the project. Only one family from the church of some 300 members came to Forest Lawn to assist in the work.

As my experience at Forest Lawn Community Church taught me, sometimes God works with small numbers of believers.

Rev. John W. Friesen, Ph.D., D.Min., D.R.S.

DENOMINATION NO. 17: THE FREE METHODIST CHURCH

As Huntington Hills Community Church continued to flourish, a church board of volunteers took over many administrative responsibilities, so as a part-time minister my workload was greatly reduced. During this time friends of mine at a local Free Methodist Church indicated that they needed a preacher strictly for Sunday duties, and asked me if I would help them out. I decided to do this since HHCC services were earlier in the day and would not interfere with the Free Methodist schedule.

I preached for the Free Methodists for about six months and appreciatively learned a bit about their church structure and operation. I also made a few lifelong friends and after reading their history, at times wondered if I would be better off as a Free Methodist!

DENOMINATION NO. 18: THE EVANGELICAL LUTHERAN CHURCH

Always one to engage in educational pursuits when available, in 1970 I learned that the faculty of Lutheran Theological Seminary in Saskatoon was offering a course on contemporary theology in Calgary. The course was being made available at the request of local Lutheran clergy but the notice said that anyone could enroll in the course. When I heard about the opportunity, I immediately I applied as a student and was accepted. I attended every class, took copious notes, and wrote a paper on the sixties "Jesus People Movement" that was invading Calgary churches at that time. Many of these folk were former drug addicts and hippies who were substituting their experiences with Jesus for former addictions. As part of my research, I attended some of their services to assemble content for my written assignment.

During the course of my studies, it became apparent that for many of my peers, taking those course was like "old home week" for them. Each of them had previously attended the Lutheran seminary in Saskatoon. I later convinced myself that my lack of connection to the old boys' Lutheran network accounted for my lower grade in the course (I got a grade of "B"), even though it was the fifth time I was taking a course on contemporary theology. Perhaps the fact that the course had a distinctly Lutheran slant threw me off!

I have a great deal of appreciation for Lutheran theology and practice. The church seems to have invented a good mix of doctrine, structure, and practice, but, depending on its national location, also has strong ethnic ties, for example, Swedish, Norwegian, or German. It is my view that one always feels more at home, if one has both ethnicity and faith in common with one's fellow adherents.

Meaningful Moments in Ministry

DENOMINATION NO. 19: THE ROMAN CATHOLIC CHURCH

I have always enjoyed visiting people in hospitals, perhaps because they tend to be very receptive to visitors, particularly visiting members of the clergy. Many hospital patients get quite lonely, weary, or depressed so they tend to be very grateful for prayers offered on their behalf.

Over the years in Calgary, my frequent visits to Calgary Foothills General Hospital brought me into contact with the staff chaplain, the late Reverend James M. Taylor. Subsequently, he and I became close friends. He introduced me to the concept of pastoral care, enrolled me in the newly established Hospital Pastoral Care Association of Alberta, and asked me to serve on its provincial board. Through James Taylor's influence, I also became involved with the Canadian Association for Pastoral Education and was named to the national accreditation and certification committee as a pastor member. Besides participating in local activities, for six years I made regular trips to Regis College in Toronto to attend meetings of the accreditation and certification committee. During this time, I worked closely with members of the PLURAS group (Presbyterian, Lutheran, United Church, Roman Catholic, Anglican, and Salvation Army), but particularly with Roman Catholics since we always met on their turf. During these years, it also became my privilege to attend mass several times and even officiate at weddings together with Roman Catholic priests.

Serving on the accreditation and certification committee meant a biannual trip to Regis College in Toronto where the meetings took place. The committee was made up of certified pastoral supervisors, theologians, and pastors with me serving in the latter capacity.

Candidates who appeared before us were usually quite uneasy because committee members could ask them anything they wanted in order to decide if they were fit to counsel people. I learned a great deal at these interviews and was often glad that I was an interviewer and not an interviewee!

When committee members broke for coffee breaks or meals, we often mingled with the theological students at Regis. Some of them were just beginning their studies for the priesthood while others were nearing graduation. I greatly enjoyed visiting with the students because, being Roman Catholic theology students, they offered an entirely different perspective on life than my students at the secular University of Calgary where I spent my career.

DENOMINATION NO. 20: THE UNITED CHURCH OF CANADA

In 1986 the work of Forest Lawn Community (Evangelical) Church was well underway with my son, Bruce, serving as pastor. A year later, my old friend, the late Reverend John Snow, Chief of the Wesley Band of the Stoney (Nakoda Sioux) First Nation, asked me to help at the local United Church on the reserve. The Morley congregation had been without a minister for several months, and by my request, my duties were at first restricted to Sundays. After all, I was holding a full-time position at the University of Calgary and would not be able to devote much time to congregational work. I was quite happy to take the position since it would give me opportunity to learn firsthand about a unique Indigenous culture, an interest that I had developed over the years with a colleague at the university.

At first, I traveled the 30 miles (48 kilometres) to Morley only once or twice a month but the position soon grew to require weekly attention. Additional responsibilities somewhat naturally evolved, including hospital visitation, baptisms, funerals and weddings, and other more social events. Before I knew it, officially I was appointed minister of Morley United Church, a part-time position I have held from 1986 to the present. My wife, Virginia, serves as Director of Christian Education, but her job description should have officially been expanded to include Sunday school teacher, choir director, social convener, co-janitor, and counselor. We did not formally join the United Church of Canada until several years later when we accepted an invitation to transfer our membership to the All Native Circle Conference of the United Church. It was an invitation we felt we could not refuse.

It seemed somewhat inappropriate to minister to a congregation and not become officially connected to their denominational affiliation. This is our present religious status, and we shall likely remain with it, partly because of our past positive experience, and partly as a tribute to Virginia's grandmother, the late Christina Lyons. She was a beautiful Christian and a devout lifelong member of the United Church of Canada.

Working in a cultural milieu that is different from that which one is used to can be quite enlightening. It affords great opportunities for learning and personal enrichment. This was certainly the case on the Stoney Reserve where we had the good fortune of having the late Rod Mark as a friendly informant. Rod, a former student of mine, was the first Stoney graduate of the University of Calgary, and the first Stoney teacher at the Morley Community School. Later he also became assistant principal and principal of the school.

At church Rod was a great help in worship as well. We sang duets together, he read the Scriptures, and helped lead congregational singing. Whenever a particularly Stoney activity took place he would inform me beforehand about what to expect and how to behave. He often interpreted cultural behaviours for me so that I might appreciate the deeper meanings behind them. As an example of this, one Sunday after church an eagle could be seen flying in a circle above the churchyard. I learned that this was a very special happening; it meant that the Creator was smiling down on the congregation.

One Sunday morning as the worship service was proceeding, a woman came into the church, tapped each parishioner in turn on the shoulder, and held out her hand. Those who were able gave her money. When she had collected as much as she needed, she left the church. In the meantime, everyone went on with the worship service as though nothing else was happening. This, by the way, was considered sharing, not asking or demanding; when someone has a need and *you* have the resources to help them, the obligation is on those who have resources at their disposal. Aboriginal chiefs are particularly vulnerable in this regard. Many times, while at Morley, I saw individuals approach my friend, the late Chief John Snow, and ask him for financial assistance. He always took out his wallet and emptied it each time. *That*, it seems to me, is *Christian* sharing!

Rod Mark passed away of a brain tumour in May 2006, at the young age of 56. About 1,000 local residents and friends attended his funeral. Rod had taught at least two generations of them, and he was a great loss to us. His teachings will live on in my classes where he will be honoured as a Christian who shared the resources God had blessed him with.

A few years ago, I was awarded a great honour in being asked to preside at the funeral of the Reverend John Snow, Chief of the Wesley Band of the Stoney Nation. John's passing was a great loss to his family, the local community, the nation. He was known across the country, as a man who with deep compassion who had a great deal of patience, even when he was publicly accused of things he did not do. His speeches and writings are quoted in many First Nations' museums across the country. He was strong believer in both Aboriginal spirituality and Christianity, and a tireless promoter of justice for Canada's First Nations.

Chief John Snow was often heard to quote from Isaiah 40: 31 (NIV): "but those who hope in the Lord will renew their strength. They will soar on wings like eagles; they will run and not grow weary, they will walk and not be faint."

I pray that my own testimony may linger long in the hearts of people I have worked with in that same spirit of encouragement. There can be no better.

PART THREE:
POEMS FOR REFLECTION

by John W. Friesen

Part Three of this book contains a dozen poems, penned by myself, most of which were published previously in one form or another.

PRAYER

Prayer:
To us is like an avenue
That opens up to clearer view
God's heavenly grace—to us endue,
His mercy rare.

Prayer:
Is like a magic, lifting force,
That stems from holy sacred source,
And helps us heartily endorse,
Our Christian fare.

Prayer:
Our Shangri-La—from daily woe,
To gain release from stress, our foe,
But yet to God, why don't we go?
Life's wear and tear.

Prayer:
Through sorrow, grief and fiercest pain,
Though vexed with fright, fear and disdain,
What is it helps so faith won't wane?
Our Father's care.

Prayer:
Is like the breath of glowing spring,

With spirit, as when children sing,
It lifts our souls, so we can bring,
To God our cares.

Prayer:
Neglect not heaven's finest gift,
God hears our call, His answer's swift,
He'll give us fast a spiritual lift,
Enjoin in prayer!

—John W. Friesen

THE MODEL PREACHER

A pastor and his preaching, are seen as close entwined,
In fact, some view the pulpit, a wee bit like a shrine.

A hearer told a preacher, his style was very warm,
He proudly told his missus, his boast was true to form.

The wife winced at his bragging, as daily he would rant,
Till one day she had had it, "to hear this more, I can't!"

As time went on, the preacher, again received a pat,
A hearer said his preaching, stirred hearers where they sat!

The word he used was "model," a preacher true to form,
The pastor liked the concept, now he was great *and* warm!

The preacher's wife grew worried, her mate was growing proud,
Not only was he bragging, his voice was getting loud.

She told him to do research, on "model," on the net,
He did, and found the meaning, was not what he'd expect.

A model is a shadow, imitation of the real,
The preacher took the message, and ended his big spiel!

Whenever you feel lofty, check out the compliment,
Your good looks and your talents, may not be heaven-sent!

—John W. Friesen

Rev. John W. Friesen, Ph.D., D.Min., D.R.S.

THANKS, I'D RATHER NOT!

A line that makes one weary, and people use a lot,
Is really just a brush-off, It's "thanks, I'd rather not!"

Can you imagine someone, whose health with illness fraught,
His doctor offers solace, says, "thanks, I'd rather not!"

Or take a needy student, whose finances are naught,
A scholarship refuses, with, "thanks, I'd rather not!"

And yet when God extends us, without our being aught,
A blessing, through some service, it's "thanks, I'd rather not!"

It seems we've got warped values, for Christ who us has bought,
May heaven's door refuse us, with, "thanks, I'd rather not!"

—John W. Friesen

THE CRISIS IN PREACHING

Too much of our preaching, I think,
Represents a mere flickering blink,
At the problems our people might nurse;
We pastors see much that's amiss,
So we scold and we holler and hiss,
Our anger we're quick to disperse!

Our pews may be loaded with folks,
Whose burdens we don't comprehend,
Because we're so busy 'gainst sin;
Our hearers go home unrelieved,
Their hearts have no respite received,
The sermon no spirits did win.

Our Lord in His preaching tried hard,
The growth of men's sins to retard,
But His words were directed to need;
The people accepted His word,
They acted on what they had heard,
Because of the way He would plead.

O Father, in heaven above,
Teach preachers to mingle in love
Their deeds and the words that they speak;
May their spirits and desires be pure,
To comfort and help, not injure,

For Christ said, "The *Bless't* are the *meek*."

—John W. Friesen

SUNDAY CHURCH

It seems to me that if God's word, I really want to know,
The thing to do on Sunday morn, is to my church to go.

Now some of us it's plain to see, have got too much to do,
The preacher doubts, but I declare, that God must know this too.

Life's little chores o'erwhelm us so, our energies they drain,
So who can blame us when we choose, from worship to refrain?

Now this may sound a little bold, but God whom we adore,
Will surely count the good we've done, and even up the score.

If that's the way you calculate, your spiritual journey here,
You've got a phony concept, and can't see things too clear!

—John W. Friesen

BLESSINGS OF WORSHIP

There are none...
If you no motive harbor deep,
Within your inmost soul,
When coming to the house of God,
With no particular goal!

There are a few...
For those who like to join in song,
And fellowship with friends,
Yet basic worth of worship true,
On more than this depends.

There are more...
Reserved for those who come to pray,
To ask of God some things,
However, worship means much more,
It's what a person *brings!*

There are many...
As those well-know who come to church,
Both to receive and give,
And what is more, they're richly blest,
And leave for Him to live!

These are for you...
If you would reap the blessings of

Real sanctuary bliss;
Then tune your heart to God today,
And worship not amiss!

—John W. Friesen

SINGING LIFTS THE SOUL

On Sunday morn we go to church,
We pray and read and sing,
And many blessings may be ours;
It bears on what we bring.

If we our hearts will open wide,
And take in everything,
Then God will surely speak to us,
When we begin to sing.

The hymns, the chants, the choruses too,
Are sung with zest and zing,
The more we put our hearts in it,
The better we all sing.

We lift our voices loud in praise,
Make sound and everything,
We clap our hands and homage give,
To Jesus Christ the King.

The Lord our worship always loves,
So let our voices ring,
Across the church and heaven-bound,
Now come, and let us sing!

—John W. Friesen

TEACHING SUNDAY SCHOOL

I'd like to see more loyalty, than what has been the rule,
Concerning an important task, *like teaching Sunday school.*

Some think that all you really need, is balls of yarn and spools,
And all you have to do is play, *and that is Sunday school!*

And other teachers I have known, think they are really cool,
They read an hour to their class, *and call it "Sunday school".*

And then there is the lecturer, who'll vocalize and drool,
While all the class sits meekly by, *enduring Sunday school.*

I think a teacher in the church, should really be God's "tool,"
A servant in a blessed role, *teaching Sunday school.*

The secret of a well-taught class, is when someone will pool
Their resources, with Christ as Guide, *in teaching Sunday school.*

In every aspect of the church, the Christian needs renewal,
And in particular it's true, *in teaching Sunday school.*

If you're involved in this great task, Just think it o'er, and you'll
Responding turn to God for aid, *in teaching Sunday school.*

It's music to a Christian's ear, and to our joy adds fuel,
To hear some youngster proudly say, *"I love my Sunday school!"*

—John W. Friesen

PARTIAL THINGS

A lesson book
And blackboard brush
Don't make a Sunday school;
A teacher with
A loving heart,
Is far a better rule!

A deacon's bench
And choral strains,
Aren't really all the church;
But people filled
With God's great love,
Would climax such a search.

To witness of
The Father's care,
Is part of Christian walk;
But earnest love
For all God made,
Surpasses any talk.

Why be content
With partial things,
When Jesus made it plain;
If you would have
Real Christian love,

Don't spend your time in vain!

The Bible take
And meditate,
Let prayer flow from your heart;
For God will bless
Abundantly,
If we will do our part!

—John W. Friesen

THE LORD'S PRAYER

Our dear loving Father in heaven above,
We hallow Thy name, in obedient love;
May Thy kingdom come, and may Thy will be done,
On earth as in heaven, as though they be one.

Give us this day, Lord, the bread we require,
Forgive us our debts, we do humbly desire;
That we may our fellowman also forgive,
And without trying temptings, we pray let us live.

Deliver us from evil, O Lord, in this hour,
For Thine is the kingdom, the glory and pow'r;
We pray that forever Thy mercies might shine,
That men might acknowledge our Father Divine.
Amen.

—John W. Friesen

A TIME ALONE

There are those times, I do regret,
My problems no solution get,
I, like Elijah in his cave,
(To whom the birds provision gave),
Feel much downcast, and right put out,
My mind is filled with stress and doubt,
And then I come alone a while,
And rid my soul of all things vile,
My God provides His inner peace,
My desperate struggles quietly cease.

When certain persons leave their place,
For worship seldom shows their face,
Another tries to steer my course,
With various tactics, even force,
My neighbors bother not with church,
For God, they show no need to search,
Then, when I come alone a spell,
My frustrations God doth quell,
Then, I remember Jesus said,
"Your conduct must be spirit-led!"

This age has parented pressures sore,
Instead of less, they're becoming more,
Our social schedules reek of plans,
We scarcely hope to meet demands,

The younger set has no recourse,
But take our path, and it endorse,
If only we could pause a bit,
And calm before our Savior sit,
That He might help us see His will,
And us with His own Spirit fill.

—John W. Friesen

A PRAYER FOR COMMUNION

Be present at our table, Lord, and may this solemn deed,
Inspire each participant, thy sacrifice to heed.

Thy presence at our table, Lord, reminds us not to judge
Another's life, lest we ourselves, be found to bear a grudge.

Thy presence in this holy deed, will make the moment right,
Without it, we might find ourselves, enacting something trite.

Be present at our table, Lord, and may we from this place,
Go happily, with blest assurance, that we have seen Thy face.

—John W. Friesen

BECAUSE HE'S GOD

The ways of man have ever shown, Him finite, frail and flawed,
Can God His love on man bestow? He can, because He's God!

Some Bible folk were vessels chose, yet idols did applaud,
But God forgave them when they asked, He did, because He's God!

The early Christian martyrs bore, the Roman's chastening rod,
Yet God was with them—gave them grace, He did because He's God!

Religions oft the Lord reject, their minds with thoughts are strewn
Of man-made gods, and yet He loves, He does, because He's God!

Believers too, the Lord deny, His holy name defraud,
But He'll renew, refill, restore; He will, because He's God!

—John W. Friesen

AN EASTER PRAYER

Eternal God, our Refuge Thou; we humbly seek Thy face,
We pray Thee, bow Thine holy ear, and grant us now Thy grace;
We recognize our weaknesses, we know that we are flesh,
And numerous are the pitfalls, by which we are enmeshed.

We need Your caring, helping hand, to guide us through this life,
For many are the lures and traps, that lead to sin and strife;
We know, O Lord, that peace will come, if we but learn to rest
On Jesus' all-sufficient grace, and give Him of our best.

It seems we know the answer, Lord, to settle our estate,
We place no stock in human powers, we need to learn to wait
Until Your Spirit, overwhelms, our stubborn, selfish goals,
And aims and plans for self decay, and love can fill our souls.

—John W. Friesen

THE BIG QUESTION

A question I frequently ponder,
But one that inspires me though,
Concerns the "beginning" of people,
And why God created them so!

One school of thought stresses purpose,
And declares that mankind must obey--
God's centralized plan for the whole race,
With no individual say!

Some persons pay court to the mere chance,
Of man being made as a thing,
Without *any* purpose or pattern,
Like a bird that is loose on the wing.

Perhaps we're confusing the issue,
And a simpler, more rational plane,
Would reveal that God wanted some creatures,
On whom He His blessings could rain!

—John W. Friesen

THE LIFE CYCLE

Infancy--the **best** of life,
In cradled innocence,
The world its torrid temptings pours
The babe makes no defense!

Childhood, and the **zest** of life,
Bursts open into view,
Searching, believing--so eagerly,
Yet sweetly, as the dew.

Youth, and here the **test** of life,
Engulfs life's precious young,
Each meets the challenge, soars away,
To earth's far corners flung!

Adulthood, the **rest** of life,
Reflects one solemn thought,
Regain what's lost, and find anew,
What's given, can't be bought.

Eternity, the **quest** of life,
Has ended, finally,
The trust betrayed, or faithfully kept,
Decided Divinely.

—John W. Friesen

A CREED FOR YOUTH

Lined up in cue to challenge youth,
And test their faith and wisdom too,
Are churches in this land of ours,
Of various kinds, and blends, and hues.

The Methodists, Episcopals,
The Baptists, Lutherans, Mormons too,
And many churches less well known,
Each claims to be the one that's true!

Each seems to have its "coat-of-arms,"
Sometimes the very name's the clue,
But often, in reality,
Their special traits they overdo!

What should inquiring youth today
Concerning faith, aspire to do?
Would it be wise to trust in fate,
And *every* structured church eschew?

Perhaps a few criteria,
At this point could be offered through,
The contemplation of what's dear,
When forming a doctrinal view.

Whatever stance you finally choose,

Blend in some love and interest too,
When you meet folks, who disagree,
Then lend an ear, and get their view.

So often in this life we find,
That faith and practice, not mixed true,
Present a picture not quite clear,
Of what it is that we should do.

Let's not our brand of creed flaunt high,
Lest we a hurtful path ensue,
Instead of furthering God's plan,
We offer man-made schemes in lieu!

—John W. Friesen

A TRIBUTE

She isn't here, she's gone to be
With God, in heav'n above,
And this same Lord it is who heals
Our wounds, with tender love;

Quite suddenly, the Lord did bid,
Her body to the sod.
The monument she left behind?
"Someone who walked with God!"

—John W. Friesen

DEAR MOM

When May rolls 'round, I think of you,
And all that you have done,
For me, and all the family,
I'm proud to be your son.

For years you struggled on the farm,
And in the city too,
But everywhere we felt at home,
'Cause we got love from you.

No matter what we found to do,
Or where we settled down,
You always prayed and wrote to us,
You ought to get a crown!

So on this Mother's Day we wish
God's best for you each day,
Because you're always there for us,
Means more than we can say!

—John W. Friesen

DAD'S 90TH BIRTHDAY

We welcome friends to this event,
A special day it is,
Our Dad reached ninety years this week,
This day is really his.

The span of time since Dad was born,
Began before the car,
Before the TV, disc and chip,
The dollar was on par!

Dad worked a store, the fields and bush,
He butchered in between,
There was no challenge left untouched,
No scars he hasn't seen.

With Mom he raised a brood of five,
And that was quite a feat,
Of course, abundance wasn't there,
But always we did eat.

The brood of five has sprung some more,
The line just seems to grow,
And if you add the whole score up,
We're forty now in tow.

Through all their travels, jobs and moves,

Our parents had just one line,
"Obey the Lord and do His will,
And things will turn out fine!"

So "Happy Birthday," Dad, today,
We wish you all the best,
But more than that, we heartily,
Thank you for your bequest.

—John W. Friesen

I MET GOD

I met God...
When in the brilliant realm of budding,
bursting spring there rose--
A fragrant soft aroma--so gloriously stowed,
In petals soft, with brisk green leaf
--that to my wond'ring eye it showed
My God had this created!

I met God...
Amid the feel of ice and snow,
when desperate railed the storm,
Among the trees, now hid beneath
great mounds of white--
High-borne their leaves, and out of sight;
left only swirling sounds of mourn;
To me this majesty revealed!

I met God...
In every season, every clime;
He's everywhere around,
And though we often fail to see
or hear His heav'nly sound,
And though it takes a little while,
a moment, and He can be found,
For our God is everywhere!

Have you met God?
Just gaze into a cradle-bed,
and note that tiny breath,
For through their entire lives,
God guards, until eventual death;
In sickness, problem, grief or pain,
the Scripture clearly saith,
"That God cares for us!"

—John W. Friesen

EPILOGUE

Looking back on fifty years of ministry in this intense way makes it seem as though most of the events I have described happened just yesterday. So I often ask myself, "What did my ministry accomplish? Who really knows? Only the Lord knows." A song I learned in the Salvation Army Sunday School years ago sometimes comes to mind containing the words, "Jesus bids us shine with a clear pure light; like a little candle, burning in the night; in this world of darkness, we must shine; you, in your small corner, and I in mine."

As Cheryl Gottselig, our wise lawyer friend of many years once said (she is by the way, a past-president of the Alberta Law Society), "You know you are not going to get out of this world alive, so make the most of it!"

Sometime ago I read the account of a rather successful minister who began his service in a small church that grew larger. He then answered the call to a larger church that grew even larger. This happened several times, and each time the church he ministered to gained more members (so did the budget, by the way). By the time he retired, the membership of the last congregation he was pastor to, numbered over 5,000. Having followed the unspoken rule about being truly professional in ministry, he and his wife were careful not to make close, primary friendships in any of the congregations they served.

You guessed it; at the time of retirement, they had really had no close friends, except for the few they had made outside of the church. Many people showed up at their retirement party, but none of them kept in contact with the minister when the party was over. The ministerial couple had obeyed the rules—they had acted professionally—and church life went on as usual in every congregation they had served.

There is a beautiful caveat to this story of a "successful" ministry. Throughout their many years of service, this couple had engaged in activities that assured them of companionship, care, and loving attention in their sunset years. They had maintained a strong family unit with their children. Despite the demands placed on their lives, they made a sincere effort to spend time together. They sought to be friends with one another and with their children, and continually communicate with one another. These efforts paid off. When this ministerial couple retired, their relationship with their children and grandchildren persisted and they never felt lonely or rejected. So while their former congregants went on with their lives, so did our heroes. What a wonderful way to end a ministry! In a sense, it was not an ending, but comprised a transference of energies to a more intimate fellowship.

May each of us, learn the lesson implicit in this story.

In 1998 I completed a Doctorate in Religious Studies degree with Trinity Theological Seminary in Newburgh, Indiana, followed by an M.A. degree in pastoral education in 2007. By now readers will be bored to learn that along with several other courses, I took a course in contemporary theology—my sixth time. I completed the degree program and graduated from Trinity with great distinction. Yes, that means I finally got an "A" in contemporary theology! Now, if I can only discover how to apply it. I hope it's not too late!

Well, there you have it.

Meaningful Moments in Ministry

ABOUT THE AUTHOR

A graduate of seven institutions of higher learning, John W. Friesen. Ph.D., D.Min., D.R.S., is a Professor in the Werklund School of Education at the University of Calgary, a position he has held for 47 years. His academic career includes elementary school in Trail, British Columbia, and Duck Lake, Saskatchewan, and high school with the Saskatchewan Government Correspondence School. His postsecondary training includes an ETA Diploma from Bethany College in Hepburn Saskatchewan, and degrees from Concord College (B.R.E.), Tabor College (B.A.), Emporia State University (M.Sc.), University of Kansas (Ph.D.), Christian Bible College (D.Min.), and Trinity Theological Seminary (M.A., and D.R.S.).

He is an ordained minister with the All Tribes Presbytery of the All Native Circle Conference in the United Church of Canada, and Minister of Morley United Church on the Stoney (Nakoda Sioux) Indian Reserve west of Calgary, Alberta.

He has authored, co-authored, or edited more than fifty books on religion, education, ethnicity, and Indigenous studies.

He is married to Virginia Lyons Friesen, Ph.D., who co-authors books with him, and they have five children, Bruce, Karen, Gaylene, David, and Beth Anne; thirteen grandchildren, Daniel, Adrian, Brittany, Rachel, Justin, Brennan, Anthea, Brina, Rebecca, Victoria, Jonathan, Andrew, and Caleb; and two great grandchildren, Keigan John, and Hannah Lily.

The Friesens reside in Calgary, Alberta. Their website is http://drsfriesen.com

The End

CPSIA information can be obtained at www.ICGtesting.com
Printed in the USA
LVOW11s1058020814

397136LV00001B/26/P

9 781460 221129